Developing
COMPUTER
SYSTEMS
REQUIREMENTS

A.K. BAKER &
THURBER

DEVELOPING COMPUTER SYSTEMS REQUIREMENTS © 2011
by J.A.K. Baker and K.J. Thurber.

ISBN 13: 978-0-9833424-0-3

Library of Congress Control Number: 2011923822

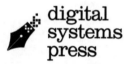

Digital Systems Press
33 Thornwood Drive, Suite 500
Ithaca, NY 14850

www.digitalsystemspress.com

Developing Computer Systems Requirements:
www.developingcomputersystemsrequirementsbook.com

CONTENTS

PART I

Chapter 1

Chapter 2

PART II

Chapter 3

Chapter 4

Chapter 5

Chapter 6

Chapter 7

Chapter 8

Chapter 9

Chapter 10

PART III

Appendix A

Appendix B

Appendix C

Appendix D

Appendix E

LIST OF
FIGURES AND TABLES

PREFACE

Based on my own experience with software application product development, the most successful projects are those in which the user requirements are clearly understood. In fact, having end users on board to provide requirements at all stages of a project—before a project begins, after concept development, after initial design, after prototype development, and after a product release—makes a marked difference in a product's success.

When developing a software application, a determination of requirements is extremely important, especially during initial concept development. Whether you are designing a system to meet a customer's stated need or designing a system for a need that an end user does not yet realize he has, articulating the requirements up front grounds the project from the customer/end user's perspective. Otherwise, you could end up developing a technology that is very interesting, but not useful to anyone—a "hammer looking for a nail."

If you are a customer, you want to make sure that the requirements that you think you have are the same as those that your design team has identified. You want to confirm that you both are trying to reach the same goals. If you are an executive or manager, you need to understand the customer or end user's requirements so that you can evaluate the proposed solution and whether or not you should advocate its implementation. If you are on a design team, you need to understand the requirements so that you know what to build! And you need to consider how the functional requirements can be met within the time and budget constraints. Those requirements must be met before you design or implement any enhancements.

Since each software development project is slightly different, it takes experience to know how to analyze a problem and develop a good set of requirements. This book contains a medley of case studies to help you get a better understanding of the range of requirements that should be considered. Examples include successes as well as some failures, from which you can learn vicariously.

The authors would like to acknowledge the contributions of Peter C. Patton, who co-wrote the original version of this book, published in 1983. The authors would also like to acknowledge assistance from those who provided technical input for the case studies in Part I:

- Noel Schmidt—Chapter 3

- Ranga Ramanujan—Chapters 4 and 5

- Jordan Bonney—Chapter 6

- Frank Adelstein—Chapter 8

- Steve Brueckner—Chapters 7 and 10

- Daniel Tingstrom—Chapter 9

In addition, we would like to thank Deanna Heaton, Christina Tomassini and Jennifer Cormier, who helped with the book's production.

—J.A.K. Baker
Ithaca, NY
February 2, 2011

PART I

Concept of Developing Computer Systems Requirements

Computer-systems architecture design is an activity at the mutual interface or intersection of hardware design, software design, and application requirements. In the late 1960s, designers began to consider the influence of system software, especially programmer-oriented languages, on hardware. The large-scale Burroughs 5500 and 6500 series machines showed early leadership in software-balanced designs. It is the hardware and software design tradeoffs that started the field of computer system requirements.

The first two chapters of this book describe the general process and technical aspects of developing computer system requirements.

CHAPTER 1

The Architectural Process And Its Relationship To Requirement Studies

This book is about determining requirements for the architecture of computing systems. Webster defines architecture as "the art or science of building; specif: the art or practice of designing and building structures." The connotation of architecture as art is particularly appropriate in the context of computing systems and their requirements. Although there is a large and rapidly growing body of knowledge about the engineering aspects of computing-system design, there has been little emphasis on techniques for determining the requirements to be used as the basis for the design of computing systems.

In the current context, the architecture design process includes activities other than those delineated by Webster. In particular, requirements analysis and specification must be integral to the design activity. In fact, in many computing-system applications, initial marketing activity involves need creation as a first—and often overlooked—step of the complete architectural process. Of course, no one of the integral activities of architecture stands alone. Requirements analysis is closely tied to the design, which is iteratively associated with logic design and software design and implementation. All of these activities are associated with evaluation, which must take place both within each activity and across activities.

Consider, for example, the focused problem of duplicating a competitor's computing system. Presumably a marketing analysis motivates the decision to duplicate, and the requirements specification is largely provided by the complete specification of the extant system. Other requirements include projected costs and additional features. The design activity could concentrate on efficient implementation, and evaluation could be required to determine how closely implementation costs match those of the target. Implementation of the copy system (which could proceed from the design and detailed evaluation) could be required to determine whether the newly implemented system meets the specified requirements, both technical and financial. Typical architectural activities include: requirements synthesis and analysis, requirements specification, configuration and subsystem design, detailed design, implementation, and evaluation. Tradeoffs cross hardware, software, and firmware boundaries at each level; and the design process proceeds iteratively.

Some decisions are simply a matter of style or insight. For example, there is no quantitative way to justify inclusion of auto-indexing address modes (see discussion of historical PDP-11 requirements in the appendix) to provide hardware support for stack mechanisms to simplify executive software data structures. Nor is there a way to know to include provenance management feature since there are not many systems that currently track provenance; it is difficult to know the value of such a feature. Likewise, at some point Intel decided to put cache memory on their processor chip sets, which used chip real estate. This again was a decision made based upon an overview of the computing systems goals. If the designer does not have an understanding of the complete architectural problem, then there is no way to show that a given proposed feature is worth the cost of implementation. The style of the resultant system will be based upon the designer's experience.

This book focuses on the problem of determining requirements and their impact on system design. Its purpose is to illustrate the process and form of requirement studies. Thus, example requirement studies from a number of military and civilian environments are described in Part II. Several important historical requirement studies are included in Part III of this book.

In a book about systems it is important to discuss what constitutes a system and how the view of a system can differ depending on whether one is the user or the designer of the system. There are no precise definitions of a system. Companies that sell memories speak of memory systems; computer manufacturers speak of computer systems; software manufacturers speak of software systems. In these cases, the word system seems to refer to the end product produced by the manufacturer.

We will define a system as a hierarchical dynamic collection of hardware and software entities. A system consists of an application-defined environment, together with the software and hardware that hosts the application. The application environment delimits and specifies the system. The software and hardware that support the system have hierarchical dynamic relationships, which together form the basis to support the application. The hardware and software are hierarchical because of the identifiable levels—that is, microcode, register level, CPU level, network strategy, database software and so on. The levels are dynamic in that in processing the application, the various levels interact to support the application.

There are several different user views of a system:

- Multi end-user system. An example of a multi end-user system is a computer utility like the World Wide Web. In this case we see general-purpose hardware and general-purpose software.

- Single end-user system. Examples of a single end-user system include a personal computer, and integrated command and control systems. Such systems have general-purpose hardware and specific software tailored to the system's function.

- Single-owner computer systems. An example of a single-owner system is a process control system such as a waste-water management system. Such systems usually have specific hardware and software.

Still another view of a system is that of the designer. In the past, since designers only focused on hardware design, the designer dealt with specific hardware and either specific, general, or—usually—no software. Today, designers have a wide variety of options available to them ranging from hardware to network system capabilities to SOAs (Service Oriented Architectures). In the future it will be important that computer architects be hardware designers as well as system designers and software architects because considering only one part of a system (such as hardware) will prove to be short sighted. To be successful, computing-system architects must be able to make realistic, relevant, and user-responsive global-system design tradeoffs. Only then will systems meet the needs of the users and customers.

Organization of the Book

Part I is organized into two chapters that discuss specific types of requirement studies and their relationship to the architectural process.

- *Chapter 1* (this chapter) describes the basis of requirements analysis and how it relates to the process of developing computer systems architecture.

- *Chapter 2* is a discussion of the general design problem and the use and definition of requirements.

Part II of the book contains a set of chapters that describe a diverse set of successful and unsuccessful case studies of requirements analysis.

- *Chapter 3* is a discussion of a radar processing system that illustrates the impact of not adjusting the design to new hardware that is provided.

- *Chapter 4* is a discussion of how an unintended use of the Internet created the need for new equipment and caused an entire new industry.

- *Chapter 5* is a discussion of a special system designed to provide high speed access to the World Wide Web in an unstable environment.

- *Chapter 6* is a discussion of a system designed to provide access for large file transmissions over long delay and unreliable links.

- *Chapter 7* is a discussion of alternative means of providing a system that is tolerant of network attacks.

- *Chapter 8* is a discussion of an automated forensic analysis product for peer-to-peer networks.

- *Chapter 9* is a discussion of a strategy and tool for managing web services.

- *Chapter 10* is a discussion of a system for online training of forensic investigators.

Part III of the book (Appendices) contains a set of historically important requirement studies and why each is still relevant today.

- *Appendix A* is an example of a requirement study of the functional characteristics of a large user group.

- *Appendix B* is a requirement study of a single application.

- *Appendix C* discusses general-purpose computer-system requirement studies, with the IBM 360 and DEC PDP-11 requirement studies as examples.

- *Appendix D* is a requirement study that extends the study in *Appendix C*.

- *Appendix E* is a requirement study for selecting a multiple processor system.

CHAPTER 2

System Requirements

A system must be designed to satisfy a need. This need must reflect the environment as well as the objectives for the system. For example, a system designed for a deep-space environment would include consideration of stringent environmental and reliability constraints on the entire system. It would also need to take into account the differences in the space environment including not just the difficult physical environment, but the effect of distance on such processes as communication path length and the ability to repair a failed part. The design process starts with determination of requirements—that is, the user's needs—from which the design is specified. It is the extension of this need that creates a market for a product. The user's needs may be broken into two categories, which are discussed further in this chapter: requirements and attributes.

Requirements

Requirements, or "musts (see Bell [1]) are the constraints that the system must satisfy. The requirements specify what the system must do. That is, any system concept that meets the requirement is a candidate solution to the customer's problem.

Attributes

Attributes, or "wants," specify either options or evaluation criteria for competing systems that meet the system requirements. Bell [1] calls attributes "objectives" and describes their evaluation as a relative maximization or minimization process. There may be many concepts that satisfy the competing architectural requirements. Attributes may be used in evaluating the competing architectures to determine the goodness of the architecture in solving the customer's problem.

Attributes may also specify options that the user desires but does not necessarily demand. The rest of this chapter will discuss requirements and attributes.

The Problem Statement

In designing a system, one must first determine the customer's needs. This involves a problem statement. Usually we will not be given a specific set of requirements, but rather a general statement of the user's problem. This problem statement describes the user's need. The specified system will be derived from this basic need and the product constraints based on the designer's industrial affiliation.

For example, if a corporation wishes to solve certain types of banking problems, based on a statement of the banking problem, the market-analysis group would first determine and specify a user need. This user need would be stated in terms of user requirements, system-cost goals, and potential market. The product-planning group would produce a system concept that solves the banking problem and allows the corporation to enter into any markets that are associated or affiliated closely with the banking problem that the corporation desires to penetrate. Finally, a product line would be established on the basis of these system-concept definitions.

In some environments, such as web-based banking, where

competition for the market is mainly fought over features, general-purpose product lines have been developed. The product-line designers will attempt to modify current products to best fit the user's need at a competitive price. When one bank gets a new feature in their system, all the other banks scramble to implement the feature in order to keep their system state of the art. This is an example of a set of requirements that continues to change. The system must continue to work and new features must be added to address the changing and evolving requirements. General-purpose systems attempt to amortize the system cost over a large user base.

In other environments, such as a special-purpose military environment, each application project officer views the solution to his own application on its own individual cost-effectiveness base. Since each such application has different requirements, each application generally requires a tailored system.

Thus, in the military environment, in contrast to the commercial environment, a system is designed specifically to fit a particular problem. No attempt is made to find the most appropriate product from the corporate-product set to fit the problem. In the commercial area most of the system-design process involves the application software, whereas in the military area the design may include both hardware and system software.

Requirements

Requirements are constraints on a system concept, the musts that any candidate system must satisfy in order to be a viable potential solution to the user's problem. Depending on the level of definition of the requirements, however, many systems that meet the stated requirements still may not be acceptable. For example, if the sole requirement were to meet a certain throughput rate, there would be many architectures that could meet the required throughput. Because of the inner-connectivity of processing elements, basic structure, or machine repertoire, however, many proposed concepts may not actually be applicable. The requirements must be very carefully defined.

The requirements are derived from the translation of the customer's functional problem definition. Typically, two types of requirement studies are *performed: requirements analysis* and *requirements synthesis.*

Typically, requirements analysis is involved with special-purpose systems or market analysis after the fact. The requirements of a system or an application are analyzed in terms of a priori knowledge about the problem derived from previous solutions. The problem environment is described to give an idea of how a new technology would be a better solution to the problem.

The Advance Multiplatform Naval Computer Study (AMNCS) is a classic historical example of a functional requirements analysis of U.S. Navy problems [2]. The AMNCS analysis tried to determine what Navy tactical requirements have been in the past and how best to apply new technology to those functions.

Requirement synthesis, on the other hand, tries to project the types of systems that will be useful in various environments in order to synthesize (create) problems or needs that could be solved with new technologies. It can be used to discover areas in which new technologies will allow a more cost-effective solution to the created problems.

A significant historical example of requirements synthesis is Hewlett-Packard's HP-35 pocket calculators. At the point in time of their introduction, the idea of a pocket calculator was extreme as the keyboard was not of a "normal" size. These were early classic examples of requirement synthesis. In this case the designers asked whether a market would develop if it were possible to build such a device. Obviously, the market developed—large numbers of people now own pocket calculators.

More recent examples of understanding the effect of a new requirement are social networks. In this case people began to develop web sites to allow them to share information with family and friends and the usefulness mushroomed. A met user need morphed into the need to figure out how to make the new concept user friendly. In this case the requirements became both a synthesis (would this concept get traction?) and an analysis problem (what features can we add to enhance the user's experience?).

There are various categories of requirements, including marketing requirements, economic requirements, technical requirements, and political requirements. An example of a marketing requirement might be that a system being designed must be capable of solving a list of designated problems. Other examples of marketing requirements include price goals, goals specifying the production cycle or product life cycle, and logistics goals.

Economic requirements typically deal with the financial constraints imposed on the system developer. For example, the nonrecurring development costs should not exceed a certain dollar amount, that the cost of spare parts for repair not exceed a certain cost, or that the manufacturers have been in business a certain number of years.

Political requirements are seen mainly by the designers of systems that require the use of off-the-shelf equipment. Designers may try to use parts that are available through their own company's manufacture, as opposed to parts purchased from other vendors. For example, a typical requirement might be that a semiconductor vendor uses its own microprocessor. In some cases, such as open software, the requirements are not driven by the normal factors of a system being specified. The requirements are driven by the community doing the work and different types of software informalisms play a critical role [3].

Political, economic, and marketing requirements may be extremely vague. Technical requirements, however, may be made very precise. They include system organization, word/byte/bit organization, hardware and software expansion capability, data-path widths, word size, memory hierarchy and memory sizes, availability of software, availability and capability of the operating system, assembly and compilation speeds, throughput speeds on specified benchmarks, type and availability of peripherals, interrupt structure and support features, instruction repertoires, local area network speeds, firewall capabilities, TCP/IP address and web address selection and utility packages. Typical web system requirements may be whether we host our web systems on our own hardware or at a hosting company and what do we select as security capabilities to prevent viruses and intrusions. Further technical requirements may include alternative throughput capabilities, input/output (I/O) capabilities, percentage utilization of resources, and cost/performance ratio. One important requirement that is typically not considered involves the type of performance evaluation and monitoring features available. This equipment is needed to allow the user to judge how well the system meets his procurement requirement, not only initially, but also as time passes.

Attributes

Since system requirements cannot be totally comprehensive and precise unless they spell out a unique system-architecture concept, attributes are introduced. It is seldom in the customer's best interest to spell out a precise system; if he does, he runs the risk of purchasing a system that is not cost-effective. A customer that buys a system in a noncompetitive environment runs the risk of paying more for that system than would be the case if there were two systems that could satisfy the requirements, so that two manufacturers could bid on the requirements. It is therefore to the user's advantage to make the requirements as definitive as possible, but, to allow for the introduction of various manufacturers' equipment in order to obtain the best price possible.

At times the architecture of the system will not be totally precise. Some features are not specifically required but are desirable, depending on their cost. In the case of Google TV, the requirements document specifies a minimum set of capabilities and intentionally allows for individual manufacturers to embellish their specific implementation [4]. Attributes are the wants (options) and evaluation criteria used to determine which characteristics make one system more desirable than another, even though both may meet the requirements. Attributes usually deal only with the detailed technical aspect of a system, and attributes in the form of desired options deal with specific system features. For example, as an option to a processor that requires an interrupt structure, one might ask that the structure not only include enable/disable by class, but also have the ability to arm, disarm, enable, and disable interrupts by level, and furnish a number of levels (such as 32)—although this is not required. In a web based system we may require both virus software and intrusion detection software to run using no more than 20% of the processor at any given time. The requirement for such features, however, may have actually been stated as follows: that the machine furnish at least four classes of interrupt with enable/disable characteristics. In the web case the requirement may have been stated in terms of a network based response time of 1 millisecond from receipt of service request. In both cases many more machines and systems may satisfy the requirement than would satisfy the attribute. Depending on how systems rank on the option list and on other general attributes, the final selection of the system can proceed. Thus attributes are the intangibles of system design. The rest of this section goes into the detailed subject of evaluation of system architectures on the basis of attributes and attribute definitions.

The following list of attributes can be used to evaluate candidate architectures. The list of attributes of an architecture must be ordered to provide their relative importance in system design. These ranked attributes may then be used to trade off alternative machine architectures: flexibility, expandability, bus complexity, network performance, executive complexity, availability, adaptability, partitioning, modularity, reliability, maintainability, manufacturability, production cost, development cost, technical risk, logistics, programmability, support-software cost, software adaptability and transferability, compatibility, and service. The definition of each of these attributes criteria follows:

Flexibility: The ability and ease with which modifications to functions and subsystems can be made. This does not include adding new functions to the system. Measures of the attribute of flexibility include ease of instruction and machine repertoire modifications, ease of support-software modifications, and ability to increase storage capability. Flexibility is a key issue in SOAs.

Expandability: The ease with which functions and subsystems can be added to or deleted from the system once it has been installed and configured. Measures include ability to increase I/O capability, available network interfaces, ability to add bus interfaces, ability to add and accept special-purpose processing elements, variety and richness of available communication techniques, and file-management-system support.

Bus complexity: The complexity of the bus structure resulting from the interconnection of subsystems and modules within the system. This is a measure of the amount of data flow within the system required to satisfy the demands of the various elements and subsystems within the system. It is possible that the complexity of the bus is larger than the complexity of the processing elements in the system itself. This should be considered in evaluating any computer system.

Network Performance: The ability of the system to connect and respond quickly to network based requests. This attribute includes whether the servers are replicated, how data is distributed, and what type of software is used on the server.

Executive complexity: The amount of code in the executive, the amount of computational overhead (in both hardware and software) required to manage and control the system and its processes, and the cleanliness of the control philosophy inherent in the executive design are all examples of the measures necessary to measure the attribute of executive complexity. Do we choose a concept based upon open source or on a commercial product?

Availability: The degree to which a system is in the operable and committable state. System availability is to some extent a measure and function of a system's inherent error-detection capability and its fault tolerance.

Adaptability: The applicability of the system architecture and its structure to a wide range of missions and applications. This measures the ability to modify the configurations such that they may be useful for more than the intended application.

Partitioning: The degree of subdivision of the system modules into functions and the layout of these functions into groups of operating hardware and software. This attribute can be used to help measure the effectiveness and degree of control the user has in the system by means of user access to bus-control techniques, I/O structures and channels, and the memory hierarchy.

Modularity: The ease with which system elements can be defined as independent functions and integrated into the system without affecting the interfaces and control of the system.

Reliability: The probability that the system will perform its intended function for a specific interval under a given set of conditions. This attribute can be measured simply as the mean times between different failure types of the system. In a safety critical system reliability is an attribute. Thus, an attribute and a requirement may be context dependent [5].

Maintainability: The ease and speed with which failures can be detected, isolated, and repaired. This is a designed-for-specification condition to facilitate maintenance or servicing. Maintainability is most easily measured by considering the system mean time to repair and the spares requirement.

Manufacturability: Can the system modules be manufactured easily, with minimum risk?

Production cost: The total cost of production start-up and replication.

Development cost: The non-recurring cost of implementing the technology, including systems concepts, support software, testing, and documentation, and, in the case of hardware, of drafting logic prints.

Technical risk: The risk involved in selecting technology and new concepts in relation to the time frame targeted for system development. Minimum risk should be calculated to occur at the time of anticipated full production to ensure the most cost-effective state-of-the-art system.

Logistics: The cost of supporting a system in the field. It is closely associated with the selected partitioning techniques, number of module types, number of technologies and logic types, dependability of the system, amount of special-purpose test-equipment tools and talents required for the support of the system, and the number and distribution of logistic depots.

Programmability: The ease with which a programmer with specified capability and experience levels can use the system. It is probably most easily estimated by considering availability of higher-order languages, compiler complexity, and services provided by the operating system. Programmability also measures the availability of the actual software that runs the system.

Support-software cost: The cost of unbundled support-software facilities.

Software adaptability and transferability: The ease involved in using software designed for a given system configuration on another system configuration.

Compatibility: User software compatibility. Can one system directly support software generated for another system? This measure includes the impact of real-time parameters and specific I/O features on the ability to run software from one system to another.

Service: This attribute is difficult to qualify but involves the availability of support service for the system after procurement.

Options that are detailed technical desires may also be rank-ordered and included in the attribute-evaluation analysis. Typical options might be inclusion of a maintenance processor, ability to upgrade to a virtual memory system, and disk-operating system availability. Obviously, detailed technical options are easier to measure than general attributes; but they are more restrictive measures of desired—but not required—capabilities.

Requirements-Oriented Design

A number of steps are involved in designing a system to meet a set of requirements. There is, however, a specific set of steps involving the use of the requirements and attributes. These steps will be summarized and discussed in this section. The actual design step will simply be described as system design so that at this point we can see how the requirements and attributes actually lead to the detailed system-design step.

The first step in requirements-oriented design is problem-analysis. This step consists of determining from the customer what the user's functional requirements are. It may involve studying the applications as they are currently implemented, trying to project what the application is or will be in the future, or trying to determine (on the basis of technology issues) what needs could be generated in the marketplace for certain types of products. The problem-analysis step provides a detailed statement of the exact problem and its functional characteristics.

The second step is the **determination of the requirements and attributes**. This step involves translating the problem-analysis functional description into detailed sets of requirements and of attributes. The requirements specify what the product system must do; the attributes specify what detailed technical options are desired for the system. A set of attributes is priority ranked for use as architectural trade-off parameters. Furthermore, at least some of the attributes will be used in evaluating proposed systems in case more than one system satisfies the requirements. The attributes should be ranked in priority order at this point to ensure objective trade-off and comparison of competing architectures.

The third design step is the **determination and description of the requirements and attributes in a specification**. Two documents should be generated. One should describe the detailed translation of the problem statement into the requirements and the derivation of the requirements from the problem statement, ending with a detailed specification of all requirements. The other, the attributes document, should specify and rank the attributes for trade-off usage and enumerate all detailed technical options.

The **system-design process** or step consists of designing delimited architectural choices. It is very difficult to map a set of requirements onto a set of architectures or to use a set of requirements to select a set of architectures. For a good evaluation of the concepts under consideration, they all may have to be designed to a level of detail that permits comparison to the requirements specification. Therefore, the design process really consists of using the requirements document and attributes document to narrow the scope of allowable choices and to narrow the number of concepts that satisfy the requirements. Evaluators screen the systems, eliminating the systems that do not satisfy the requirements. Architectural descriptions are generated and furnished to the attribute-evaluation step for all remaining architectures.

The attribute ranking is used in an attribute-evaluation step to list the architectures in descending order of their satisfaction to the attributes. Then a number of systems that all satisfy the requirements—and are ranked in order of priority of satisfaction of the attributes—may be selected and bids solicited from manufacturers. Alternatively, in designing a system from scratch, a system concept that satisfies all of the requirements and is one of the systems that ranks high on the attributes should be selected for detailed design.

Requirements and attributes make the design process manageable. They cut down the number of choices one must make by clearly delimiting these choices. Obviously, the process must be iterative. Changes in technology, cost considerations, and so on may cause changes in the requirements or attributes specifications. Further, the use of requirements and attributes splits the design goals clearly into "musts" and "wants" (options). The effect of the process is continually to narrow the choice so that the designers can quickly focus on the problem. Thus the requirement/attribute/problem analysis continues to refine the general spectrum of architectures down to a single architecture that is best suited for the application. This is the architecture that is ultimately designed. A complete collection of papers discussing the details of this design concept is available in Thurber [6,7].

References

1. Bell, C.G. *Designing Computers and Digital Systems Using PDP-16 Register Transfer Modules*. Boston, Digital Press, 1972.

2. Shen, J.P. "Advanced Multiplatform Navy Computer Systems (AMNCS)." NELL/TR1847, September 1972.

3. Scacchi, W., Understanding the Requirements for Developing Open Source Systems, IEE Proceedings-Software, 149(11), pp 24-39, February 2002.

4. MIPS Technologies, Inc., Preparing for Google TV, Document Number: MD00789, Revision 01.07, July 23, 2010.

5. Murray, D.P. and Hardy, T.L., Developing Safety-Critical Software Requirements for Commercial Reusable Launch Vehicles, 2nd International Association for the Advancement of System Safety Conference, Chicago, IL, May 14-16, 2007

6. Thurber, K.J. *Tutorial Computer System Requirements*. IEEE Computer Society Press, 1980.

7. Thurber, K.J. and Patton, P., "Computer System Requirements," Lexington Books (D.C. Heath) Lexington, Massachusetts, 1983.

PART II

Case Studies

As previously illustrated, computer-systems architecture is a design activity at the mutual interface or intersection of hardware design, software design, and application requirements. Originally computer architects designed hardware (based mostly on what was technically possible rather than on what was needed by ultimate users), which system programmers managed to program and application designers managed to employ for the satisfaction of real-world problem requirements. In the early 1970s designers began to consider the influence of system software, especially programmer-oriented languages, on hardware. In 1964, the large-scale Burroughs 5500 and 6500 series machines showed early leadership in software-balanced designs, but now evensmall computer architectures show this influence. For example, in 1981 Intel introduced the Intel iAPX-432 which was designed with the Ada language and its environment in mind. Now many other chip designs address operating-system requirements.

By the time application requirements are brought into consideration in the design of a system of any size, the hardware and system software usually appear to the end user as constraints. The only variables for which designer decisions may influence ultimate system architecture and performance may be the programming-language and operating-system configuration. Thus the utility of the final system may depend on the degree to which the programming language of choice suits the application; the degree to which the machine code that language generates is able to take advantage of any hardware architectural features desirable to the application designer; and, finally, the flexibility of the operating system in accommodating a multiplicity of concurrent processes not necessarily imagined by its designers.

In this book we are addressing the balance of the three-legged stool of hardware, software, and application requirements. It is not always possible for the end user to influence hardware and software design issues directly. To a large extent this is a consequence of the fact that hardware design was technology driven, and then down only a few alternative paths. A second factor, almost as important, was the extremely long lead time from design concept to application in the field. Today, technology has matured to the point that many alternatives are possible, and lead times are so short that the feedback signal from the application field to the design laboratory can be distinguished from the noise. Thus, it has become important for the hardware designer, so long insulated from the user by time and software, to be able to make some sense of this feedback signal—that is, the requirements.

We present a number of examples and case studies in chapters three through ten of how system requirements were developed. It is unlikely that every reader will be interested in each example, but anyone interested in the application of digital-computer technology to real-world problems will find several helpful examples for understanidng the feedback problem. Of necessity, our examples were chosen from our own experiences as computer designers and consultants; thus there has been an arbitrary selection criterion. The experienced reader will be able to supply similar examples from his or her own experience. We have also made up pseudonyms for some of the companies and people involved in these actual case histories in order to protect the guilty (as well as the innocent). The reader should carefully consider the lessons illustrated.

CHAPTER 3

Speed Improvement in a LAN Environment

We start with a simple problem and see how the requirements have to be met by a design change. This example illustrates one of the big problems in trying to understand requirements: How do you know what will happen when you try to translate from requirements to a system?

This will be the first of four chapters that describe the impact of requirements for performance on the design of specialized communications systems. In this case, the problem is the performance [1] of a radar tracking system. The system consists of a radar processor that takes in raw radar data and puts out a track (a tuple describing the xyz coordinates of an aircraft). Each aircraft detected by the radar generates a tuple for every pass of the radar. The tuple must then be passed to a track processor for display on a radar scope.

In the days before distributed processing systems, such a system (Figure 3-1) was quite limited in capability and in fact, in many cases the radar data was fed into the same processor as the one that performed track management. In such a system, the capacity of the system was extremely limited in the number of tracks that could be processed because of the fact that the same processor had to both process the radar data, the track data and tracking algorithms, and the display processing. The idea of separating some of the processing into multiple processors connected on a local area network (LAN) was very attractive as it could provide a large speed up of the system thus allowing more planes to be in the air space (Figure 3-2).

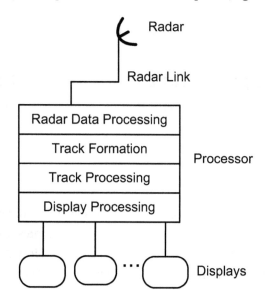

Figure 3-1: Centralized Air Traffic Control System

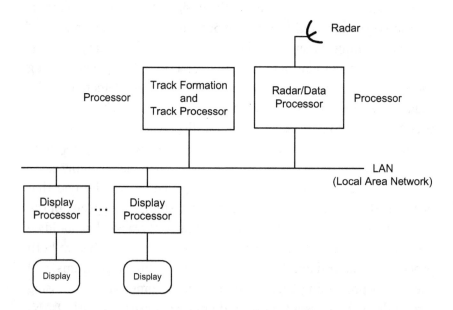

Figure 3-2: Distributed Air Traffic Control System

In this case the design problem was very simply stated: replace one slow processor that performs radar, track, and display processing with two processors, one for radar and one for track and display processing connected by a LAN. (Actually this is an abstraction of the actual problem. The problem has been simplified for this chapter so that we can focus on the real problem encountered.)

What happens next is classic. In building the new system the design team puts in two very significant high speed processors and a high speed LAN. They port their software, make some changes and bring up the test system. The performance of the new system is dismal. In fact it is less than the performance of the old system even though every part of the system is at least one order of magnitude faster than the old system.

Consider a functional abstraction of the old system. The old system contained a direct high speed link from the radar to the processor. When a radar buffer was input, the processor was interrupted and the track's xyz coordinates processed and sent to the track processor. The new system could not even get the tracks sent over to the track processor at the rate the old processor received them. Yet every part of the new system was state of the art and extremely capable as well as fast.

The design team was sent back to do measurements of the performance of all parts of the system. The result: the radar processor was doing its job and performed perfectly, the track and display processor had the same result and the LAN was performing at speed. The design team could not find the source of the problem through testing because every part of the system operated properly. The design team was confused.

Consider three essential facts about the system that must be understood in order to make the system perform properly. First, the processing of the radar results in a set of individual tuples which are delivered individually to the track processor. Second, the design team decided to port the existing software, making minimal changes to the ported software. Third, the way the LAN communication system worked was like any modern communication system: it had a layered set of protocols that were invoked as the information went from the source to the destination, with each layer adding information for the control and routing of the radar data.

Eventually the lead designer figured out how to explain the problem. The problem was really simple and its solution was also very simple. The requirement to separate the processing did not specify how the software had to be changed but left that to the designers. The designers had taken the software and simply ported it. Thus, each track was being sent to the track processor on the LAN. Since as the track information was small in size in terms of total bits, but the information that controlled its transfer was large in terms of bits, by sending each track in a separate packet, the effective rate of transport of the LAN was destroyed because the overhead information necessary to contain and transmit the radar xyz information was nearly 100 times as large (in bits) as the radar information for a track (Figure 3-3). Since each track was being sent separately the high performance LAN had less performance than the direct link by a huge factor.

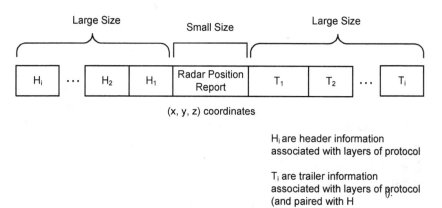

Figure 3-3: Packet structure illustrating relative size of information fields

The requirements specified that the information had to go from the radar processor to the track processor. It did not specify that each track had to be sent separately. When the tracks were collected into groups in the radar processing and sent to the track processing the performance problem went away.

This is an example of designers not paying attention to critical aspects of the design. When the requirement specification does not tell designers how to design the solution, but instead tells them the function to be performed, naive designers may go ahead and just build the system like they did before without thinking about the ramifications of the new parts of the design.

This is an example of what not to do in a packet-based system: Do not send short packets unless you absolutely must, as the impact on performance is severe.

Reference

1. Thurber, K.J. and Schmidt, N.E., "LAN Requirements for Air Traffic Control," Proceedings, 1987 Fall Joint Computer Conference, Dallas, TX, October 25-29, 1987, pp. 85-88.

CHAPTER 4

The Impact of Upper Layer Protocols on Performance

Another example of requirements analysis leading to a need for a new solution to obtain increased performance is that of large file transport over the internet—WAN (Wide Area Network) acceleration.

In many cases businesses today have multiple offices distributed over a large geographic distance. If the offices are in close proximity the amount of delay between offices is minimal (in the sense of how long it takes for a packet of information to go from one location to another). This is the exact case that the Internet protocols were designed to accommodate. Fairly minimal delay and highly reliable lines for communication are the Internet's basic design parameter.

But, what happens if you were to change one of the parameters. For example, what if we were to postulate a system with a long delay? What would the performance result be?

Consider a business that has two offices: one in the United States and one in Japan. If you use the Internet to send a large file what will happen? In general the result has two parameters that impact performance: the speed of the slowest link in the chain of links between the United States and Japan, and the longest delay experienced between the two sites. The performance between the two sites will be based upon the performance you can get through the slowest link, but the delay may cause the performance to degrade substantially due to the timeouts built into the Internet protocols. This is illustrated in Figure

4-1 where we have a satellite uplink, a satellite downlink, and two internet connections. In this case any one of the links can be a bottleneck. The protocols governing the overall transmission may also cause performance problems if they were designed to work over symmetric links without long time delays.

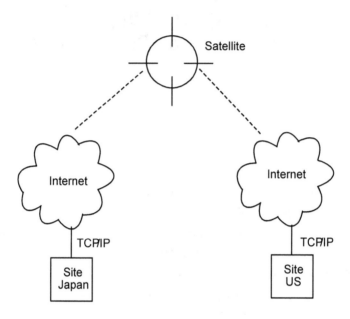

Figure 4-1: A simple geographic Internet system

This is a serious problem and the requirement becomes one of trying to fill the slowest link in order to transfer the maximum amount of data. But the timeouts work against your ability to fill that link.

This is a real problem whether you are going over high speed fiber or a satellite. In the case of a satellite, there may be an asymmetric quality that must be considered; short commands may be uploaded at one speed and data downloaded at a different speed.

The requirement to transport large files over long delays has not only created new technology solutions but has created an entirely new industry. The basic solution generated by this requirement is that of building a new hardware box (one must sit at each end of the system) that sits at each end and takes in information as if the endpoint were the final destination or source. Between these two points we can substitute a new communication protocol that does not adhere to the basic Internet protocols between the two end points, but instead uses a special protocol designed to optimize transmission between two points that contain a long delay. These boxes then try to fill the links between the two endpoints with as much information as possible. This is illustrated in Figure 4-2.

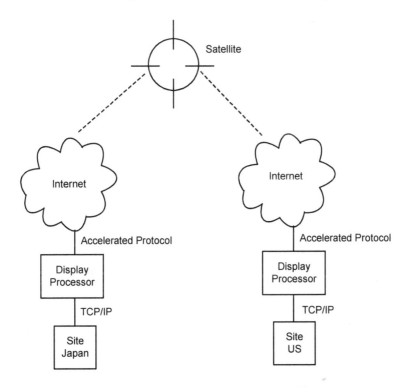

Figure 4-2: Geographic Internet system with accelerators

The use of the Internet for purposes not considered in its original design (transmission of large files over long distance) has not only led to new design trade-offs, but has led to new products and a completely new industry, packet accelerators (sometimes referred to as WAN accelerators).

CHAPTER 5

Development of a Communication System for an Unreliable Environment

In Chapter 4, we discussed how the requirements (and thus the solution) for a communications system would change from that used by the Internet if we had to operate in an environment where one of the key design principles of the Internet were changed; i.e., if delays increased substantially. In this Chapter, we will look at another system in which an assumption changes [1].

Consider a system that is to operate from ship to shore over a satellite. In this case, the time delay is large. In the previous chapter we found solutions to solve the time delay problem. But when operating on a ship, there is also the problem that the ship is communicating over an unreliable satellite link. Not that the satellite link itself is unreliable, but the pitch and roll of the ship makes the satellite connection unreliable because it becomes out of sync with the antenna on the satellite. The requirements for a more reliable system could be stated as follows: Develop a TCP/IP Stack for the Windows Operating System (NT 4.0 or later) that is optimized for wireless communication links. The stack should have parameters that are modifiable so that the stack can be optimized for a particular link—slow speed satellite, high speed satellite, and high bit error rate. Further, the system needs the ability to set up and close the satellite connection quickly.

In this case, the ultimate question is whether such a system can be built. There are a series of technology challenges associated with such a system. The first issue is that since the satellite link is expensive, you do not want to keep the link open for long periods of time when nothing is happening. So a requirement is to build a fast set-up and tear-down protocol. Additional requirements are to detect when the antenna loses contact with the satellite, and a means to queue data so that when the link comes back up, the system can send as much data as possible.

The traditional approach for implementing mobile Web access over satellite links uses a PPP dial-up connection to an on-shore remote access server (RAS), as shown in Figure 5-1. Once a PPP dial-up connection has been established, Web clients on mobile platforms and Web servers based on the shore can communicate over it using HTTP, which in turn operates over TCP/IP. For secure Web access, the Secure Socket Layer (SSL) protocol may be interposed between HTTP and TCP/IP.

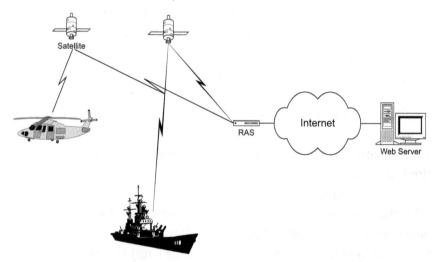

Figure 5-1: Web-based access to on-shore information resources from offshore platforms

A mobile client's Web interactions can be divided into the following steps or phases:

1. Establishment of a dial-up PPP connection to the RAS

2.   Access of one or more Web pages

3.   Teardown of PPP connection

The user has to pay for airtime from the time that physical connection to the RAS is established, in Phase 1, to the time that this call is terminated in Phase 3. However, the satellite link may be used only for a small fraction of the time during Phase 2. This happens when a Web transaction initiated by the user causes data transfers between the Web server and the Web client over the PPP link. The link remains idle between transactions. Up to 95% of the time may be wasted due to inactivity.

A solution that is a software-based solution was developed to enable the cost-effective and efficient implementation of mobile Web applications over satellite links. The concept relies on software that runs on the mobile client as well as on the access point connecting the fixed network to the satellite link. It implements three novel capabilities: a dial-on-demand router, a tunable TCP/IP stack, and Web proxies. The roles and functions of these three software components are described below. Figure 5-2 shows the overall structure of the software.

Dial-on-demand router: This function resides in the data link and network layers of the protocols stack of Figure 5-2.

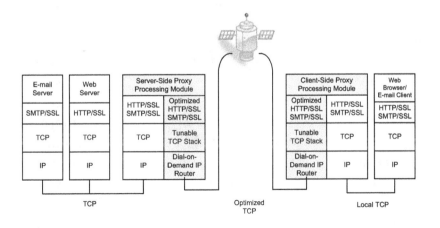

Figure 5-2: An architecture for mobile web access over satellite links

The Dial-on-demand router's primary function is to establish a virtual network connection, on an on-demand basis, between the mobile client and the remote access point when it senses network traffic generated by interactions between Web client and the Web server. The built-in intelligence within the dial on-demand router determines when the satellite link reaches the idle phase and tears down the connection to save airtime charges during these idle periods.

Tunable TCP/IP Stack: This implements satellite link specific optimizations to the standard TCP/IP stack to deliver significant improvements in the latency seen by end users for Web transactions between the mobile client and the onshore web servers. A novel approach was used for fine grained tailoring of TCP protocol functions and parameters that allow for the optimization of TCP performance for different types of satellite links; such as narrow-band GEO links, narrow-band LEO links, broadband GEO links with narrow-band reachback, and bi-directional broadband LEO links.

Web Proxies: The approach relies on the interposition of two Web proxies between the Web client and the Web server, i.e., a client-side proxy and a server-side proxy.

The client-side proxy resides on the mobile platform and the server-side proxy resides on the on-shore fixed network. The transport layer connection between the two proxies is tailored to optimize its performance across the wireless satellite link. This includes TCP/IP optimizations as well as optimizations to the SSL protocol that are needed to minimize connection set-up and data transfer latencies of these transport layer functions. In fact, this approach even allows for the replacement of the TCP/IP protocol between the proxies by any other protocol tailored for satellite environments.

The major benefit of the proxy architecture described above is that it requires no changes to legacy Web clients and Web servers. Such clients and servers may use the standard TCP/IP stack to communicate with the client-side and server-side proxy respectively. Transport-layer optimizations are pushed to the proxies that use the optimized stack. In addition to optimizing the transport layer connection between the proxies, techniques such as application specific data filtering and data caching can be implemented within the proxies to further minimize data transfer latency for Web transactions and thereby further reduce airtime for satellite links.

In the case that your goal is to build a critical system, such as described, you must break the requirements down into parts that you can then implement. In the case above, a number of interacting piece parts were necessary to actually implement the deployed system.

Reference

1. 1.R.S. Ramanujan, S. Takkella, and K. Thurber, "MobiWeb: An Approach for Mobile Web Access over Satellite Links," Proceedings of the 2000 IEEE Aerospace Conference, March 2000.

CHAPTER 6

Development of a Communication System Accelerator

Experience in disaster emergency response (DER) systems has made reliable bandwidth important. Unfortunately, the off-the-shelf Transmission Control Protocol (TCP) implementations perform poorly (or not at all) over the data links that connect United States based command centers with forward–deployed response units. Poor TCP performance over DER links is due to longer data-transfer times and squandered bandwidth. In contrast to the systems described in previous chapters, there can be long delays (due to satellite links), unreliable links (due to unstable vehicle dynamics) and unreliable links (due to use of unreliable radio transmissions from the satellite platform to field radios).

Though a number of TCP optimizations have been introduced, they have yet to collectively address the unique bandwidth, latency, loss rates, asymmetry, and security characteristics of such environments. But such a product is possible and is described below.

Overlay routing has been proposed as a method for providing a degree of determinism over an otherwise non-deterministic Internet. Overlay routing can dramatically improve end-to-end performance when multiple paths exist, but it provides no improvement when the weakest link in a path is the final link in the path, and no alternate path exists.

Another approach is to develop a dynamically self-tuning TCP/

IP stack (TCP-D-Stack) that adapts its data-transmission algorithms to the constraints imposed by the available data links. The adaptive TCP/IP stack cooperates with a Path Characterization Service (PCS) that provides control plane information about the alternative paths between the source and destination of a given TCP data flow.

Combined, the adaptive TCP stack and the PCS are expected to yield an order-of-magnitude improvement in TCP performance between land-based posts and remote units. Since TCP-D-Stack requires no modification to the interior routing infrastructure of a given Internet, investment in existing communication infrastructure is completely preserved. The TCP-D-STACK approach can also be incrementally deployed, thus minimizing the disruption to system availability.

This strategy can be implemented via a judicious tuning of the Microsoft TCP stack after extensive experimentation. The TCP-D-Stack software structure and its rationale are described below.

While TCP/IP has been increasingly refined over the course of the past two decades, the refinements have largely been targeted at the diverse link characteristics of the commercial Internet. Links used for disaster emergency response, however, commonly possess three properties not found in the commercial Internet, and these properties severely limit standard TCP/IP performance and are critical requirements that must be taken into account to make sure that an emergency response system can have good performance:

- Asymmetric links

- Packet loss rates exceeding 1%

- Intermittent link disconnections

TCP-D-STACK is an innovative approach for implementing a Microsoft Windows-compliant TCP/IP stack that overcomes the limitations of TCP in dynamic wireless environments. TCP-D-STACK augments the control plane of TCP with novel mechanisms that enable it to:

- Discover and select the most desirable network paths

between end-points in a path-diverse and network-address-diverse environment

- Elicit an explicit characterization of the network paths between two end points

- Automatically perform path-specific tailoring of the protocol's control mechanisms and control parameters for optimizing the performance for each TCP session

Underlying the TCP-D-STACK approach for optimizing the performance of TCP over DER networks are three innovations which allow TCP-D-STACK to meet the requirements of this unconventional environment:

1. Augmentations to TCP control-plane signaling mechanisms that enable a stack to obtain an explicit characterization of the network paths between the two end points of a connection and to select the most desirable of these paths for data transfer.

2. A dynamically adaptable TCP/IP stack implementation for Microsoft Windows platforms that enables fine-grained tailoring of the TCP control mechanisms and parameters governing the operation of these mechanisms on a per-connection basis to accomplish path-aware performance optimization of a TCP connection.

3. A virtual overlay path (VOP) mechanism that enables application-transparent operation of a TCP connection in a multi-homed host environment with address and path diversity.

The TCP-D-STACK approach is based on the notion that if the characteristics of the network path(s) between the end points of a TCP connection were explicitly made available to the TCP stacks at these end points, then an appropriate tailoring of the stack's control mechanisms and parameters can be performed "on the fly" to optimize the performance of the connection. This represents a dramatic departure from the conventional approach for implementing TCP/IP stacks for the Internet environment where the stack attempts to implicitly determine the characteristics of network path by monitoring operational parameters of the data plane, such as packet losses.

Therefore, conventional TCP/IP stacks are designed to implement the conservative mechanisms for congestion control and loss recovery recommended by the Internet Engineering Task Force (IETF) for TCP operation in the shared Internet. Changes to any of these mechanisms are understandably approached with extreme caution since a flawed design could wreak havoc on the shared Internet. The DER network environment, while presenting unique challenges to the operation of TCP, also presents an opportunity for embedding the network with services that can provide TCP with explicit knowledge of network paths. The idea underlying the TCP-D-STACK approach is to leverage this opportunity to optimize TCP communications between end-points on the DER network. For communication with end-points that are not on the DER network, conventional stack mechanisms and parameters may be employed.

A hypothetical use of such a system would be a 1-gigabyte file transferred from a land-based FTP server to a forward–deployed Emergency Response Unit (ERU) over an asymmetric path consisting of a 16 Mbps Global Broadcast Service (GBS) forward link and a 2.4 Kbps narrow-band satellite link reach-back channel. Then the information could be forwarded to the field units via an ad hoc radio network.

Because of standard TCP implementations' congestion-avoidance mechanisms (slow start, fast retransmit, etc.) transferring the 1-gigabyte file takes at least an order of magnitude longer than the theoretical minimum transfer time of approximately nine minutes. Furthermore, adding 20-30% packet losses may in fact keep the file from being delivered at all. Thus, TCP is unable to make bandwidth-efficient use of the GBS link.

Suppose the TCP stacks were made aware that the forward network path from the FTP server to the client had a provisioned bandwidth of 16 Mbps; a loss rate of up to 30%; a path latency of 250 ms and an MTU of 1KB; and that the return path to the server had a bandwidth of 2.4 Kbps and a path latency of 250 ms.

This knowledge of the network path between the server and the client can be used to tailor or tune the TCP/IP stack for the connection as follows. First, the receive window is set to its optimal size, i.e., the bandwidth delay product for the path (1 MB). Second, the slow-start mechanism can be disabled altogether and the connection can start with a congestion window equal to the advertised receive window (1 MB). The sender can pace segments at the forward channel data rate to prevent burstiness in network traffic. Third, the receiving side's stack can be tailored to send ACKs at a rate that prevents ACK congestion on the low-data-rate reverse channel.

Finally, for congestion control, one may use a novel receiver-driven approach where the receiving stack continually monitors the data loss rate. Should it exceed the upper threshold of the path loss, i.e., 30%, the receiver exponentially reduces its advertised window. Should the loss rate fall below the threshold after the reductions, the receiver may linearly increase its advertised window.

With the above optimization, and assuming no congestion, the transfer of the 1-gigabyte file in the above example would approach the ideal transfer time of about 12 minutes as opposed to over two hours for a conventional TCP/IP stack. In practice speed ups of over 180 times were achieved via this technique.

Figure 6-1 depicts the notional DER network environment that is targeted by the TCP-D-STACK approach. The figure shows a forward–deployed DER IP site, i.e., the ERU LAN, connected to the CONUS-resident IP site via the DER Internet cloud. The ERU LAN is a multi-homed IP site that connects to the DER Internet via multiple service provider links, e.g., a 128 Kbps dial-up satellite link, a dynamically provisioned GBS link, and a high-speed terrestrial link. This is analogous to an enterprise network connected to the Internet via multiple ISPs.

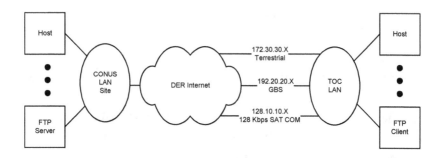

Figure 6-1: Notional DER network environment for TCP-D-STACK

The multiple service provider connections to the DER Internet provide the ERU LAN with path diversity as well as address space diversity for communication with remote networks. Each service provider provisions a different subset of the DER Internet's address space for use by hosts within the ERU LAN (e.g., 128.10.10.X, 192.20.20.X, and 172.30.30.X) for the three links shown in Figure 6-1 and may provide a different quality of service. A host on the ERU LAN can be configured with one or more IP addresses derived from the three disjoint address spaces assigned to this site. Microsoft Windows facilitates multi-homing of a host by allowing assignment of multiple IP addresses to a network interface. Thus, multi-homing of a host does not require multiple network interfaces for the host.

To meet the system requirements, we replace the standard TCP stack in a host with a new stack, i.e., the TCP-D-STACK stack, and introduce a new network service called the Path Characterization Service (PCS). Together, the TCP-D-STACK stack and the PCS implement innovative control-plane augmentations for TCP to enable communicating hosts to select and use the most desirable network path between them in an application-transparent manner. Furthermore, the control-plane augmentations enable the communicating stacks to elicit the characteristics of the network paths between the hosts. This information is then used to perform path-aware tailoring of the control mechanisms and the control parameters of the stack, at run time, to optimize the performance of the data transfer over these paths.

This example illustrates the extent that one may have to go to in developing an aggressive system to meet a specific set of requirements.

In this chapter and the three previous chapters, we have provided an insiders view of an increasingly aggressive set of communications requirements and the impact on the system design of the communications system. In the next chapters, we will look at other types of systems and their requirements.

CHAPTER 7

An Attack Resistant System Strategy

The goal of this case study was to provide improved survivability in IP networks via technologies to enhance the likelihood of a system's ability to persist under conditions of extreme attack and/or degraded performance.

In a network-based system, the basic building blocks consist of the processing nodes which can be servers or workstations. Nodes are connected via links that are provided by the communication subsystem. Routers and firewalls, as well as intrusion detection equipment, can reside in the system or in sub networks of the system. The processing nodes (both servers and workstations) may also contain software that can be used to detect and mitigate a variety of attacks, such as viruses.

The requirement is to specify a means via which the nodes and thus the system can be made to be fault tolerant to an attack. Historically, fault tolerance has been defined as being able to recover from a hardware or software failure. In this case, we are concerned about recovery from an attack. For the remainder of this chapter, we will describe a node that can recover from an attack as an Attack Tolerant Node (ATN).

There are a number of strategies that can be employed to try to satisfy this requirement. These varied strategies depend upon the type of equipment or manufacturers with which the designer is familiar.

One strategy (if you manufacture routers of firewalls) is to develop a system that will allow the router or firewall to isolate the node until it can recover or repair itself.

A different strategy (if you manufacture intrusion detection devices) is to develop techniques to isolate the node based upon detection and isolation of intruders.

Further strategies may involve the use of active honey pots to confuse the attacker.

In this chapter, we will detail a completely different approach— that of trying to keep the node itself running during an attack that gets through all of the above types of defenses and their attendant strategies. This approach is modeled upon early fault tolerant systems such as the Tandem Non-stop computer but uses modern virtual machine technology along with hardware redundancy to achieve its attack fault tolerant capability.

Information systems are susceptible to attack and compromise. Isolation of the network is not always an acceptable response to detected cyber attacks. For critical missions, it is necessary to be resilient to cyber attacks. Networks designed to withstand cyber attacks are known as *resilient* or *survivable* networks. A survivable network is capable of carrying on (in a perhaps degraded state) during an attack, continuing to provide (potentially limited) critical services.

Human reaction times are very slow in comparison to the speed of cyber attacks, which can occur in milliseconds. A survivable network must be able to react to attacks more quickly than can be accomplished with manual intervention. Survivable systems therefore require an automated response capability, so the network can dynamically respond to threats.

The insight behind the ATN concept is that not all nodes in a network are equally important to a given system. In many large-scale networks, some nodes are immediately critical to success whereas other nodes play a secondary role. We call network nodes that host one or more essential services *mission-critical nodes*. For example, in Figure 7-1, three nodes have been identified as critical for the mission of data analysis and dissemination. A network without these nodes would be unable to provide any level of service whatsoever; conversely, a network with only these nodes would be able to provide at least a minimal amount of service.

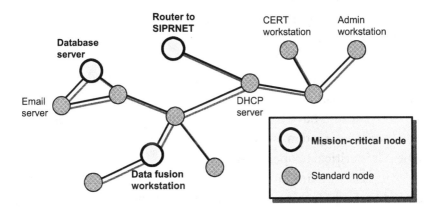

Figure 7-1: A network in which mission-critical nodes are identified for replacement with Attack Tolerant Nodes

The Attack Tolerant Node (ATN) is used to replace nodes hosting mission-critical services in a network. Networks equipped with ATNs should be resilient, enabling critical processes to operate despite attacks on the node or impacts on other parts of the network. ATN is a hardware-based solution with customized software—a small rack of servers used to replace an existing mission-critical server or workstation.

ATNs are intended as drop-in replacements for existing nodes on operational networks. One of their innovations is to break down communications with the rest of the network into specially defined transactions, which are used as synchronization points.

ATNs are designed to be resilient to attacks, operate reliably despite compromise (to a threshold level), and be easily re-deployed after being irretrievably compromised. The methods used to achieve these capabilities include redundancy, sandboxing, synchronization, check pointing, and restoration. While survivable against network attacks, the ATNs design is particularly effective against more insidious host-based attacks; i.e., attacks that compromise a server or workstation.

Central to the ATNs operation is the notion that the running state of a program (and its storage) can be captured between discrete Input/Output (I/O) transactions. This is the common paradigm for database operations. A primary innovation for ATNs is the extension of the transaction concept to other types of programs, primarily services but eventually to include other types of network accesses such as sessions.

ATNs would have key application capabilities in a system such as a brokerage system, a banking system, or a military application where it is critical to operate at all times.

An ATN contains an ordered group of n (where n is an integer) cloned Virtual Machines (VMs) that host the node's critical service and act as transaction sandboxes. Incoming transaction requests are dispatched to the first worker VM in this group. After each transaction completes, the next VM in the chain is synchronized with the previous one, resulting eventually in an active record of the previous n transactions. That is, only the first transaction in the series will have been executed on the last VM, and all n transactions of the series will have been executed on the first VM. After n transactions are complete, incoming transactions are temporarily suspended while the integrity of the VMs is checked with an Intrusion Detection System (IDS). If the VMs remain uncompromised, all VMs are backed up, or *check pointed*, and then the next n transactions are processed. If any VMs are compromised, they are automatically isolated and their state saved for later forensic analysis. Replacement VMs are immediately started from a warm backup, i.e., a recent checkpoint. The source of the transaction that caused the compromise is (optionally) blocked at the ATNs firewall to prevent re-infection.

In an example, an attacker uses a database transaction to trigger a zero-day exploit that compromises a database server and its hot standby server (which was susceptible to the same exploit because it had been mirroring transactions). The attacker installs a root kit onto both machines, allowing him to launch a variety of denial-of-service (DoS) or stealthy data-centric attacks against the C2 data. The presence of the root kit is immediately detected, but the servers must either be taken offline for repair or allowed to run while under control of the attacker. Neither alternative is acceptable.

To implement a survivable network the database server would be converted to an ATN. This would increase its ability to survive and attack as the attack would be neutralized by the ATN properties and operations can safely continue. The compromise and root kit are isolated within one or more of the ATNs sandbox VMs. The VMs are rolled back to clean images from warm checkpoints and the ATN continues to service incoming transaction requests. The compromised VMs' disk and memory state are provided to a response team for forensics analysis, so the exploit can be characterized and the vulnerability patched. The source address of the malformed transaction is blocked at the ATNs firewall, preventing re-infection from that vector.

Attack Tolerant Node Architecture

Physically, an ATN is a small rack of servers connected by two networks. The true architecture emerges when one examines the VMs hosted by each server (Figure 7-2). The heart of the ATN is an ordered group of "worker" VMs that execute transaction requests from the operational network. Although there are nine VMs shown in Figure 7-1, the system can scale to provide fewer or more to improve performance. The worker VMs are regularly monitored for compromise; when they are "clean" they are backed up and when they are "dirty" they are restored from a recent (warm) clean backup. This is how an ATN maintains service when attacked: by verifying post-transaction integrity using VMs as sandboxes, and by eliminating compromised worker VMs and replacing them with fresh ones.

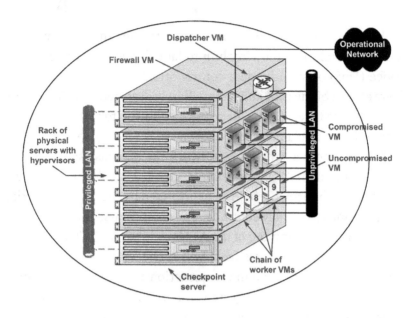

Figure 7-2: Attack Tolerant Node (ATN) provides the ability to survive attacks through its sandboxed VMs

A firewall provides an adaptable first line of defense. Next, a router dispatches connection and transaction requests to the lead VM. Each VM acts as a sandbox. VMs are monitored for compromise using host-based IDSs and are check pointed regularly. While VMs remain uncompromised, their states are synchronized within one step (transaction) of their neighbors. When a set of VMs becomes compromised, it reconstituted from a recent, clean checkpoint (i.e., warm backup). The privileged LAN is a network that isolates the ATN's critical functionality from potential compromise. The ATN checkpoint server residing on the shadow network securely stores checkpoint VM images.

The ATN has a single address on the operational network; mediating between the worker VMs and the operational network is a firewall and a router, or *dispatcher*. The firewall provides an adaptable first line of defense for the ATN; when an attack is detected the firewall can be automatically reconfigured to block future attacks from the same source after the worker VMs are restored. The dispatcher stores and forwards transaction requests and responses. It forwards transaction requests from clients to the worker VMs, but not to all workers simultaneously (as discussed below). It sends delayed responses back to clients because it must wait to determine whether transactions were attacks or not (avoiding the problem of "rolling back" the clients). By forwarding transaction messages serially, the dispatcher forces the VMs' services into deterministic behavior, avoiding the complication of race conditions between simultaneous requests.

There are a number of potential strategies to use the pool of sandbox VMs to balance ATN resiliency with performance. One strategy is to line them up into a "pipeline," in which each transaction is executed on each VM serially. That is, the first transaction is executed on VM1, and then during the next "time step" the first transaction is executed on VM2 while the second transaction is executed on VM1. When the first transaction in a sequence is executed on the final VM, all VMs are paused, checked for evidence of attack, and restored as needed. This pipeline approach allows us to perform the security checks and create backups less frequently (rather than after every transaction), yet still provides us with a set of discrete checkpoints that are only one transaction apart so we can "roll back" the ATN to the appropriate point.

The clean checkpoints of all VMs are stored on the checkpoint server. This host is not connected to the VMs, but rather to the hypervisors hosting the VMs on a privileged network. The ATN's critical processes (synchronization, integrity checking, check pointing, and restoration) are executed by the hypervisors, so that under normal operation (which includes "normal" attacks; i.e., attacks on processes or their operating systems) the critical processes are safe from compromise. In the unlikely event that an attacked VM can escalate privilege and compromise its hypervisor, the entire ATN must be restored from a *cold* backup, i.e., its initial configuration. This restoration would involve swapping the hard drives of the physical servers, which requires manual intervention but can still be accomplished within minutes. The compromised hard drives would be made available to a response/forensics team for analysis.

Note that the operation of an ATN assumes the existence of a means to detect attacks, i.e., an IDS. For the case of an attack on service *availability*, (a network or host-based DoS), this is a trivial requirement, since a DoS that is not easily detectable is a rather ineffective attack and does not require resiliency. More subtle is an attack that quietly compromises a node for the purpose of stealthily exfiltrating or altering data. Such IDSs do exist, and it is upon these that an ATN relies to detect attacks on a node's *confidentiality* and *integrity*. In fact, because the ATN's server hypervisors have a higher level of privilege than the VMs, IDSs executed from the hypervisors would provide ATNs with a higher level of assurance than typical IDSs could achieve.

The idea of an ATN addresses the requirement listed at the start of this chapter with an extreme design of the node itself, assuming that all of the normal defenses have been exhausted. The idea of the ATN is an example of developing a special processor to try to overcome vulnerabilities that may be resident in a system.

CHAPTER 8

A Strategy for Automated Forensic Analysis

In this case study, the goal is to provide a tool to help law enforcement investigate usage of peer-to-peer file sharing software in an automated time-efficient manner.

Peer-to-peer (P2P) file sharing software allows individuals to scan and download files stored on other computers. Figure 8-1 illustrates how individuals share and distribute information and the complexity of tracking the source of information.

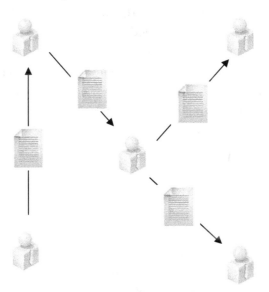

Figure 8-1: File sharing in a P2P network makes it difficult to track the source of illicit material

P2P technology has been widely used in cyber crime ranging from financial to child pornography. Forensic labs report that child pornography crimes represent approximately 80% of their caseload. And because of the number of existing P2P networks, such investigations are extremely time-consuming; thus, an automated tool is required.

Since P2P applications are widely used in child pornography cases, they represent a major source of evidence on computers that are under investigation. After law enforcement seize a target computer, a digital forensic examiner often needs to rapidly identify the kind and number of files that have been shared through P2P technology. This analysis process is manually intensive and time consuming as investigators must determine which types of P2P clients were used, identify all associated files and extract information from those files. This typically requires the investigator to research the specific P2P software to determine the location on the disk where the software stores files, the names of configuration files, and their content. Of particular interest are the configuration parameters (user name, password, servers used), log files of any transactions, and the downloaded (or shared) files themselves. An investigator must gather, categorize, and analyze all of this information by hand. In addition, the investigator may need to obtain some secondary software (beyond the investigator's normal tools) that translates a log file into a human-readable format. Clearly, this is a time consuming process.

Major Requirements: Automated, Integrated and Extensible

Investigators need tools that *automate* this process and bundle together all of the information relating to each P2P network. While some automated tools exist, they are very limited in scope: they operate on only one P2P client and perform only one analysis task (for example, translating an "activity" log file into a human readable format). Since investigators operate under tight deadlines, an *integrated* tool supporting multiple P2P clients would greatly help investigators by reducing the time required for the analysis process. The automated tool should scan for the presence of P2P software and report information relevant to each P2P client that is found.

Currently, there are a few dozen networks and several dozen P2P programs in general use on the Internet. While a small handful of programs comprise the majority of P2P usage, each program is slightly different. Because new P2P clients and networks frequently appear, an effective P2P analysis tool must be *extensible* to support additional P2P platforms as they arise. It is essential that the analysis tool must allow knowledge of new P2P software tools to be added through the use of "plug-ins" or configuration files.

P2P Marshal

This section describes P2P Marshal, a tool that meets the requirements for automated forensic analysis of peer-to-peer usage.

P2P Marshal shows the investigator the files that have been downloaded from a P2P network as well as related information such as the P2P servers used. It shows relevant configuration information, such as the user's name and a list of servers that were used, and displays the log file in a human readable form. P2P Marshal supports multiple P2P networks and is easily extensible so that new network descriptions can be added. P2P Marshal is a stand-alone tool, requiring no additional software.

P2P Marshal can perform a detailed analysis of eight of the most frequently found P2P networks. Different P2P networks leave different artifacts. And any individual P2P program may leave only a subset of its information as evidence on a disk. P2P Marshal creates a list of evidence that these programs leave on a disk, such as information stored in log files indicating possession or distribution of illicit material.

A key component of P2P Marshal is its configuration file that specifies details of different P2P networks and clients. The details include ways to detect the presence of a particular client (e.g., by looking for a particular file or directory name), data file locations, log file formats (e.g., how dates and files are represented), and patterns to match in P2P configuration files (e.g., user names and passwords). The configuration file contains separate specifications for each supported P2P client. The configuration file allows the generic P2P Marshal analysis mechanisms to work on a particular instance of a client. P2P Marshal's analytical engine supports a wide array of networks and clients. P2P Marshal developers can extend the tool, adding support for new clients by specifying new client definitions in the configuration files.

P2P Marshal's user interface is designed to be easy to use. It is a windows-based scheme in which a set of tabs is provided, with each tab showing the results of information gathered for a particular P2P network (Figure 8-2). The information on each tab is presented in a standard way (for example, user name, server names, downloaded file list, and activity log).

P2P Marshal acquires all of the files related to a particular P2P configuration in a forensically sound way. P2P Marshal works on a disk that has already been imaged and mounted as a logical volume. This presents several advantages. First, the initial imaging process is unchanged. Second, because P2P Marshal works from a copy of the data, it cannot damage the evidence. Third, existing tools, such as EnCase, FTK, or The Sleuth Kit, can be used to retrieve deleted files, which then appear to P2P Marshal as just another directory. P2P Marshal does not support the decryption of encrypted files directly, as that is a separate, difficult challenge better addressed by cryptographic tools. In general, decryption programs must be run on the disk files before P2P Marshal is run.

P2P Marshal generates a hash (e.g., MD5, SH-1) of all required files. These hashes not only preserve the files' integrity but can also be used to search databases of known files for matches.

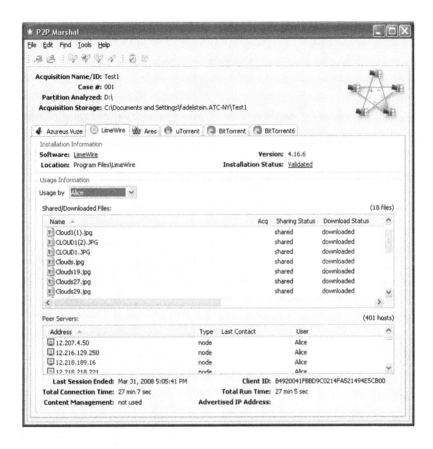

Figure 8-2: P2P Marshal's easy-to-use interface

P2P Marshal interprets acquired files and displays relevant information (for example, user name, downloaded files, dates, user's IP and supernode IP address). Once the files have been acquired, P2P Marshal presents them to the investigator in a human-readable form, translating log files as needed. Reports may be generated in several formats, such as HTML or rich text.

Conclusion

We have described the requirements and resulting automated tool to enable time-efficient investigation of P2P usage. The benefits of P2P Marshal include:

- Increased productivity in laboratory and field investigations

P2P Marshal operates in a laboratory environment on an image of a seized computer as well as on a live computer in the field and provides a large speedup of the investigative process. The steps to gather all P2P usage, previously taking several hours, now completes in minutes.

- Easy to use

P2P Marshal's user interface is easy to navigate and contains the information that an investigator needs to review. A key feature is the thumbnail browser, which helps to reduce face time of the investigator with offensive materials.

- Forensically sound

The automated processing of gathering P2P evidence is accomplished in a forensically valid way. Specifically, P2P Marshal gives consistent and accurate results for every run and the process is well documented. This documentation helps an investigator explain the automated process in the event that the accumulated evidence must be used in court. Each investigator action is captured and logged with sufficient detail. P2P Marshal's log is human-readable so that it can be used to support an investigator's testimony in court.

- Helpful report generation

Investigators can annotate and mark evidence for inclusion in a report. P2P Marshal can generate highly configurable reports in several formats. Investigators have an option to insert their agency's logo.

More information on P2P Marshal can be found at www. P2PMarshal.com.

CHAPTER 9

A Strategy for Managing Versions of Web Services

In this case study, the goal is to provide a tool to help Service Oriented Architecture (SOA) developers and web services administrators easily manage deployment of new web services or changes to existing services so that inconsistencies can be identified beforehand.

Requirements for Web Services Management

Service Oriented Architectures (SOAs) provide the loose coupling and re-usable component architecture necessary for large-scale information systems within the DoD and commercial enterprises. DISA's Net-Centric Enterprise Services (NCES) program provides military capabilities by interacting with services through a SOA approach [1]. Fast decision-making can be mission critical, and providing reliability of services by maintaining backwards compatibility for clients is important. In the Navy, the Consolidated Afloat Networks and Enterprise Services (CANES) initiative promotes exchange of information between tactical and operational units through SOA [2]. CANES uses an Enterprise Service Bus (ESB) with a large number of services categorized into enterprise services, core services, basic information services, infrastructure services, and network support services. With so many services interacting together, it is vital that upgrading the services is done in a maintainable and efficient manner while providing the least system impact for military clients.

Yet upgrading a SOA service by hand can be costly and inefficient as the system evolves and complexity increases. Complexity can arise in multiple scenarios. One such scenario is when multiple versions of a service are maintained using a single, evolving interface. In this case, service developers can preserve old operations and append new ones, but the data types in the interface must also change over time; old data types must remain as well as the new ones. Having multiple versions of data types which represent the same abstract entity can be confusing for clients who might have to map between the different versions and it is also confusing for developers who have to maintain backwards compatibility for every new revision [3]. Further, the cost of maintaining and supporting these old versions grows with each revision, and may quickly become prohibitive.

Another scenario is when developers use multiple interfaces to separate the versions of services into different instances. The problem here is that as the versions grow so does the number of services and cost of system resources. Also, moving older clients to the newly available versions can be difficult.

It is very common in SOA environments to have services which depend on other services. Emerging developer tools, such as Yahoo! Developer Network [4] and Yahoo! Pipes [5], which create "mashups" of data sources and services on the web, are becoming extremely popular. While these composite services create exciting new functionality for end-users, the services can break easily if the dependency links are not managed correctly. As services evolve, the complexity of the dependency chains increases dramatically as translation services are added to the mix. The cost of maintaining old versions and translation services can only be justified if it is easy to assess their criticality to the overall mission or enterprise goals.

Whether a service is SOAP-based or RESTful, backwards-compatibility immediately becomes an issue when a developer unilaterally changes a service, unaware that he is creating conflicts with requestors who still need to use the older service. Some examples of non backwards-compatible changes include modifying the set of service operations and revising a complex data type. Clients who cannot immediately adapt to the new service will be stuck.

When non-backwards-compatible changes are made to a service, there are a few possible approaches to take which lower the cost of integration efforts. One approach is to keep all of the original operations. This approach is not feasible in large distributed systems since the number of operations and data types is unwieldy and the service developer is forced to continue providing deprecated APIs.

Another approach is to create an intermediary service for older requests/responses to pass through. The "older" requests can be identified by utilizing XML namespaces to represent versions in the WSDL description or other SOA interface document. This intermediary service could act either as a translation component by translating older requests/responses to current service requests/responses, or it could act as a standalone legacy service.

In large distributed systems where services depend on each other, the management of service revisions and impact analysis of new revisions can be difficult and costly. A system is needed to efficiently manage large distributed service data flows and multiple service versions.

Web Service Interface Revision Environment

In order to address the requirements, we introduce the Web service Interface Revision Environment (WIRE), a system designed to efficiently manage version problems in a large distributed network of services. WIRE is a framework for web service version control, including versioning support for WSDL, SOAP translation components to translate requests from one service version to another, and a management system to efficiently manage a large distribution of services and assess the system impact by analyzing the services' dependencies. The WIRE framework is extensible and scalable to many SOA enterprise environments.

The major features of WIRE are:

1. A standard framework for maintaining web service version information. Currently, there is no standard framework for SOA service version control.

2. The capability to assess system impact by showing service dependencies and usage statistics. WIRE visually displays the conflicts involved with revising a service. By examining the usage statistics and system impact ratings, the administrator is able to either resolve or ignore potential conflicts when services are revised.

The WIRE product works as shown in Figure 9-1.

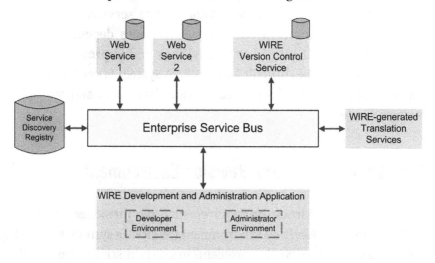

Figure 9-1: Overview of the WIRE components

There are two components of the WIRE framework: the WIRE Version Control Service (WVCS) and the WIRE Development and Administration Application (WDAA). WIRE-generated translation services provide backward compatibility for clients that must use an old service interface; the ESB automatically routes requests through the translators when appropriate. Users of WIRE fall into two main classes: service developers and service administrators in large-scale distributed information systems. (In smaller organizations, the developer and administrator roles may be shared.)

WIRE Version Control Service

The WVCS is built as a standard SOAP-based web service that stores version information and dependencies in a database backend. After developers edit existing or create new version information, the data is sent to the WVCS. When administrators request a list of dependencies for some particular operation of a particular service, the WVCS responds with the corresponding results.

WIRE Development and Administration Application

The WDAA consists of two environments: one for service developers and the other for service administrators. In most enterprise environments, the developer roles are different than the administrator role, but in smaller deployments they could be the same person.

The *developer environment* allows developers to maintain version information as they make changes in their services. This environment also allows developers to add version information to existing services which have not been previously used with WIRE.

The *administrator environment* allows service administrators to efficiently assess the system impact before removing services in a system-of-systems context. They can assess the impact by visually examining the dependencies for a particular operation in a dynamic graph drawn by WIRE. The graph also contains other beneficial data such as *usage statistics* for each dependency (as gathered by the

ESB) and user-supplied system impact ratings to help the administrator determine the appropriate action to take when deprecating services.

Customers can plug the WVCS into their existing ESB, and immediately start using the WDAA. WIRE product is platform and ESB independent; WIRE works in many different enterprises. By making the task of maintaining version information easier for developers, the goal is to make developers more inclined to save version information with every service that is created.

WIRE supports service developers and service administrators:

Functionality for the service developer

- WIRE visually represents a service given the service's interface (e.g., WSDL), and WIRE's functionality is built into the interface. This allows developers to edit version information, change/delete/create operations, etc. WIRE maintains all of this information automatically.

  WIRE's validator ensures that version data created in a WSDL via some other software (e.g., a text editor) works in the WIRE system. WIRE uses an XML schema for version data to be store in WSDLs. The WIRE validator reads the schema to determine if version data stored inside of the interface is valid.

Functionality for the service administrator

- WIRE helps service administrators by providing tools to show service dependencies and enough useful information about the dependencies so that administrators can assess the system impact efficiently before making changes to existing services. Dependency information is created by the developers. Developers can use WIRE to parse other SOA-related documents (e.g., BPEL, WSLA) available in their environment into service interactions and augment WIRE's dependency information with representations of these interactions.

WIRE has support for showing dependencies per-operation and per-service and for showing dependencies per-parameter value range. For instance, if an operation getFoo(int x) in service A calls service B, and service B only gets invoked when x is in the range of [0,100], an administrator might know that it is unlikely that getFoo requests will have parameters in that range, and therefore the administrator also knows there will be a much smaller impact if his service B is deprecated or removed. Besides ranges of integers, there can also be regular expressions to match string-based parameters as well. This per-parameter range dependency feature is useful for services which *branch* to other services depending on particular parameter values.

We will implement functionality to dynamically express dependency graphs visually in a multi-domain context. Figure 9-2 shows an example of 3 domains. In this scenario Domain 1 and the Domain 2 have services that are indirect and direct dependencies on Service 8 in the Domain 3. All of the services are per-operation, and the services on the left call the service operations on the right as denoted by the arrows.

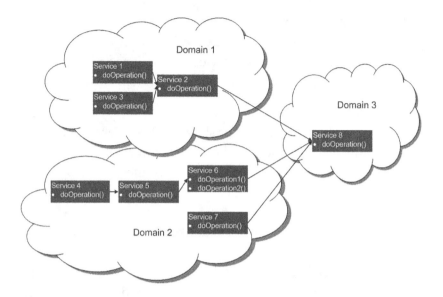

Figure 9-2: Sample visual dependency graph showing how the services in different domains are connected

WIRE Benefits

The WIRE framework design has the following architectural benefits:

- *Loosely-coupled middleware*—WIRE requires no modification to existing system components or architecture. Users should be able to plug WIRE into their existing ESB infrastructure and immediately gain the benefits of version management.

- *ESB Independent*—WIRE does not depend on specific ESB software. The only requirement is that the ESB provides a means of collecting usage statistics for particular web services, and most ESBs provide this functionality out of the box.

- *Scalability*—The WIRE framework can be scaled to many services, and even potentially multiple ESBs connected together in an enterprise network.

The WIRE application has the following customer benefits:

- *Agile versioning impact analysis* is available through the WIRE administrator environment.

- *Version control management* helps service developers, either on the same or different ESBs, collaborate together to produce reliable services that can continue to work over time even through system changes. Also, similar to source code version control systems such as SVN and CVS, WIRE can automatically manage certain version fields (e.g., date modified, author, and version number) to reduce cost for developers.

Conclusion

Using WIRE will decrease the expense and time required to maintain web services which work reliably in spite of changes to other services with which they interact in a system-of-systems environment. In particular, WIRE benefits two groups of users: service developers and service administrators. Service developers benefit because WIRE allows them to smoothly maintain service version control (as of November 2010, there are no standard version control systems for web services). Service administrators benefit because WIRE will help them to assess the system impact before launching new revisions. WIRE provides a visual dependency graph to show how services depend on each other and also providing helpful data such as usage statistics and domain information. Thus service administrators are able to make better informed decisions when deprecating or revising services. WIRE does not depend upon any particular ESB software or require modifications to existing ESB components or architecture.

References

1. NCES Users Guide Version 1.1/ECB 1.220 of 20 April 2007.
2. CANES SOA Vision and Plans. Gary Shaffer. Program Executive Office C4I, PMW-160. April 11, 2007.
3. Josuttis, N. SOA in Practice: The Art of Distributed System Design. O'Reilly. 2007.
4. Yahoo! Developer Network. **http://developer.yahoo.com/**
5. Yahoo! Pipes. http://pipes.yahoo.com/pipes/

CHAPTER 10

A Strategy for Comprehensive, Cost-Effective Online Training in Computer Forensics

In this case study, the goal is to provide a cost-effective system for online computer forensics training to enable students to efficiently and effectively learn computer forensics skills.

Online Digital Forensics Training

Military, government, and commercial enterprises are all vulnerable to criminal misuse. Digital forensics is the science of investigating digital devices, transmissions, and storage media to acquire and analyze evidence related to an incident or crime with the goal of providing solid information to assist decision makers in an organization, military, or legal context. The discipline is essential in addressing rising cyber crime rates, and acting as a deterrent to insider threats by providing attribution. There is need for advanced training capabilities to help students rapidly acquire the specialized skills needed to perform digital forensics investigations.

Requirements

As physical crime rates are falling, computer crime is skyrocketing, with new stories appearing weekly in the media. In addition, cyber criminals have a relatively small chance of being caught and successfully prosecuted. Military, government and commercial enterprises are susceptible to cyber attack due to its reliance on computer network infrastructure and the asymmetric nature of cyber warfare. Disruption of commercial enterprises due to cyber crime and cyber attack costs millions of dollars per year. The consequences of an attack on a military or government network can be catastrophic. There is an immediate need for trained personnel to respond to computer attacks, yet limited training time, limited budgets, and continual rotation of personnel makes this imperative difficult to meet.

The scientific discipline required to investigate and counter cyber threats is *digital forensics*: the investigation of digital devices, transmissions, and storage media (e.g., computers, networks, hard drives) to acquire and analyze evidence related to an incident or crime with the goal of providing solid information to assist decision makers in an organization, military, or legal context. The field of digital forensics originally focused on investigation of inactive storage media, but more recently live or *rapid* forensics capabilities have become part of the discipline [1,2]. Rapid forensics refers not only to the speed of the investigation, but to the ability to acquire short-lived *volatile* data from running systems. Rapid forensics capabilities can be critical in many military and commercial situations, where response time is an important factor and immediate access to compromised systems is possible.

Two significant military applications of rapid digital forensics are to the *insider threat* and *advanced persistent threat* (APT) problems. Insider threats are cases where malicious individuals working inside an organization who are trusted with access to sensitive information. Insider threat is considered one of the most critical-to-address yet difficult-to-solve problems in computer security. Since digital forensic investigations can provide attribution to an inside attacker's actions, such investigations provide accountability and act as a deterrent. Advanced Persistent Threats (APT) are cases where a sophisticated attacker has gained a foothold inside an organization. Such an attacker can maintain a stealthy, long-term presence to continuously exfiltrate or alter sensitive data. Rapid digital forensics can be used to detect APT compromises and profile the intrusion, allowing for successful remediation and removal of the intruder.

Digital forensics knowledge, techniques, and decision-making are complex and difficult to teach. An advanced training capability is needed to teach students the specialized skills, processes, and tools used in rapid digital forensics investigations. Such a capability would combine theory and practice in a realistic context, as in the example of modern pilot training. Military pilots absorb information through lectures and books (which include visualizations such as aircraft diagrams and maps), but also gain practical experience in flight simulators, where they have a safe, realistic environment to practice skills and learn from inevitable mistakes. Exposure to a variety of simulated scenario types enables learners to employ case-based reasoning [3], applying previous lessons to new situations.

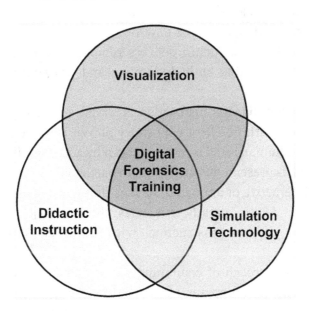

Figure 10-1: Effective training in digital forensics would incorporate didactic instruction, simulation, and visualization technologies

As the flight simulator example illustrates, training in the kinetic realm is fairly advanced. No capabilities of equivalent sophistication exist in the cyber realm for the field of digital forensics. The need is for a modernized training system that leverages the natural symbiosis of the proven learning techniques of didactic instruction, visualization, and simulation into an integrated environment that supports digital forensics training (Figure 10-1).

Due to the complexity of the discipline, current training methods for effective digital forensics are instructor-intensive. The use of pedagogic automation and online accessibility can enable the training to be available anytime, anywhere, greatly enhancing cost effectiveness by eliminating travel and scheduling concerns.

The Alcuin System

Alcuin is an integrated e-learning environment for automated training in the field of digital forensics that combines traditional didactic instruction, hands-on environmental simulation, and visualization technology. Alcuin delivers remote learning content by seamlessly integrating both declarative and procedural teaching methods.

Traditional didactic instruction is a well-established teaching methodology with excellent expository power. However, for many subjects the human mind is more engaged by and retentive of information that is presented visually, and in particular by visualizations that are interactive or animated, such as those made possible in the digital era. Alcuin greatly enhances the learning process by augmenting didactic instruction with advanced visualization technology.

Alcuin's approach of combining didactic and visual materials provides a powerful means of presenting information. However, according to constructivist learning theory [4], learners are not passive recipients, but actively construct the knowledge that they acquire, and the more realistic and authentic the learning environment, the more likely it is that learning will transfer to the work environment. Alcuin therefore includes realistic simulation technology to provide trainees with interactive hands-on training within goal-based hands-on exercises.

Any successful online training system requires automation to support the mission of round-the-clock availability. Existing Learning Management Systems (LMSs) provide automated trainee assessment with static didactic content. Alcuin automatically evaluates trainee performance in hands-on exercises that are conducted within a virtual Forensic Lab Environment (FLE). Alcuin employs the cognitive apprenticeship model [5] providing personalized one-on-one tutoring while the learner is actively engaged in the activity being taught. Following this model, Alcuin monitors a student's progress through one or more exercises as it tunes the amount of instructional "scaffolding" provided.

Alcuin incorporates a realistic learning environment for dynamic tactical exercises, increasing the chances that what is learned didactically will transfer to real life forensic challenges. By using virtualization technology, Alcuin actually provides a training environment of real computer systems and is technically not a simulator. The virtual FLE is therefore full-fidelity, enabling the cyber-equivalent of "live fire" exercises. These exercises employ real attacks and real forensics investigation tools (any existing digital forensics tool that runs on Windows or Linux platforms can be plugged in to Alcuin).

Alcuin uses an LMS to deliver traditional didactic content to trainees and integrates the LMS with its virtual FLE to provide a seamless training experience. Novel visualizations of forensic evidence that the trainee finds during exercises are used to assist the trainee's learning process. The visualizations provide three views of the data: a table, a timeline, and a topologic view. These views are dynamically generated and interactive. The table view incorporates the trainee laboratory notebook, which requires the student to show his work during an exercise.

Alcuin is available online and accessible using a standard web browser, so the trainee does not need to install specialized software. Its automation allows trainees to access and use it any time of day. Instructors set up an exercise in advance, and can review trainees' performance after exercise completion.

Training content is presented to trainees in two windows, allowing the trainee to conduct training exercises while interacting with a virtual tutor. (If a trainee is using a small screen such as that on a laptop, he may not be able to view both windows at once.) As the training exercise progresses, the automated tutor employs a combination of didactic instruction and visualizations to provide exercise and lesson information, ask and answer questions, and give hints and feedback. When critical events happen in either the simulation or the tutor, the appropriate window alerts the user by flashing or popping up in front of the other window.

Alcuin incorporates an interactive visualization for correlating data. A timeline is used to represent forensic events temporally, and a network diagram represents those same events topologically. As events on the timeline are selected, evidence on the network map is highlighted. Similarly, as events on the network map are clicked, they become highlighted on the timeline. By clicking on an event, the user can drill down to obtain more detail, which is imported from the trainee's own Alcuin Notebook. As the user discovers more evidence during his forensic investigation, he adds new events to this electronic notebook.

The role of an instructor is to select and assign learning units to trainees, and review the results of student performance. Learning units include combinations of didactic instruction, visualization, and simulation exercise. Learning units run automatically and are graded automatically, without the presence of an instructor.

Didactic Content and Format

Alcuin's didactic content is delivered to trainee browsers using a standardized interface and format. Alcuin uses Distributed Learning

(ADL) initiative's Sharable Content Object Reference Model (SCORM), a DoD-mandated standard. SCORM appears to have the widest adoption among LMS platforms and is fairly stable and backwards-compatible.

Visualizations

Alcuin uses dynamic abstract visualization to highlight the relationships between complex data sets. The visualization presents forensic evidence gathered by the student (objects and events) using three perspectives, or views, that are dynamically linked together:

1. an electronic lab notebook that displays the raw data in table format,

2. a timeline that presents the absolute chronology of events, and

3. a topologic view of the computer network that shows how objects and events are related spatially.

The visualizations help orient the trainee on how the forensic evidence is interrelated in the dimensions of type, time and space (respectively). This orientation assists the trainee in the high-level competencies of documentation, completeness, data interpretation, situational awareness, data correlation/synthesis, and deductive reasoning.

The Alcuin Notebook

Digital forensic professionals must maintain good notes of their investigations. Alcuin's Notebook provides a convenient way for trainees to take notes, and provides an underlying structure that allows Alcuin's automated assessment capabilities to parse and evaluate the trainee's notes for correctness.

From the perspective of forensic practice, an investigator's notes are his work product and his basis for analysis. The Alcuin Notebook interface can be used to define or enforce the separation between the collection and analysis portions of the forensic process. Many rapid forensic investigations are team oriented, and from this perspective Alcuin's shared Notebook is a convenient method for communicating findings between team members. From a teaching perspective, the Notebook is an ideal place to put scaffolding in the form of forensic artifact hints. From an evaluation perspective, the Notebook remains an essential tool to gain insight into the student's reasoning. Finally, from a visualization perspective, the Notebook represents a jumping off point from which to build the other dynamic views of information entered by the trainee.

Figure 10-2: Notebook front-end with integrated Timeline

Timeline

Timeline creation is an integral part of incident response and is used by professionals in the field to keep track of major findings and develop insight into the overall incident under investigation. Alcuin's Timeline (shown in Figure 10-3) illustrates the absolute time relationships between events. For example, when a time interval is selected on the timeline, all events in that timeline are highlighted and displayed on the notebook and topologic views. A slider on the timeline can be dragged right and left to "play" the events back on the topological view. A zoom in/out feature allows trainees to view events at different levels of granularity.

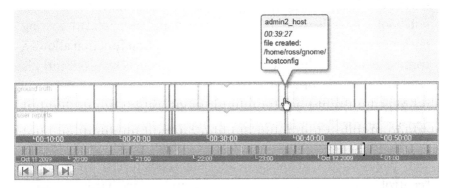

Figure 10-3: Concept drawing of enhanced Timeline visualization

Topology

Alcuin's Topologic View is based on a diagram of the computer network under investigation inside the exercise scenario. As with the Timeline View, evidence from the Notebook is displayed in the Topologic View by selecting the desired Notebook entries. For example, objects located on specific hosts are displayed as color-coded icons in the corresponding locations on the network diagram. Network connections and packets between two hosts are displayed along the lines connecting those hosts in the diagram.

Virtual Forensic Lab Environment/LMS Integration

In Alcuin, the LMS (which provides didactic and visualization content) is integrated with the virtual training environment, (the Forensic Lab Environment, which provides hands-on exercises), interleaving didactic/visualization content with simulation exercises, allowing events from each component to trigger events in the other. Such events may include key decision points within the exercise, questions asked by the student, or feedback provided by the Alcuin automated tutor.

The Notebook's SQL backend allows the trainee powerful yet easy-to-use options to filter and sort the evidence displayed in the notebook view. To simulate a physical pen-and-ink notebook, the notebook allows users to create new entries and to append to existing ones, but not to delete entries. Instead, a redaction function allows a trainee to indicate that the trainee no longer believes the old entry is relevant, accurate, or valid.

When a trainee selects forensic evidence in the Notebook, it appears on the Timeline with an appropriate label.

Alcuin hosts common components of each system (web servers, web pages/scripts, databases, and file repositories) on a single "control" server to facilitate interaction and reduce hardware overhead. State maintenance/control services runs on the shared control server. The virtual FLE is an independent module hosted on a dedicated rack of servers. Figure 10-4 shows a component-based view of Alcuin's integrated architecture.

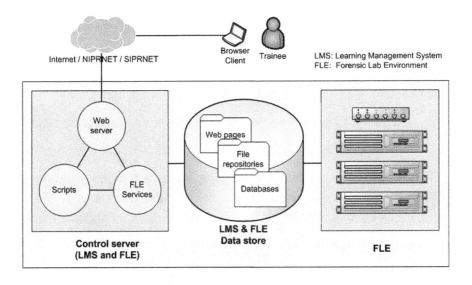

Figure 10-4: Alcuin component architecture

The visualization components are modular, with a loose coupling to other components within Alcuin. This allows for the greatest flexibility, reuse, and ease of development and testing.

Training Modules

An Alcuin Training Module includes:

- didactic content, served by Alcuin's LMS component, which includes

  - text and figures explaining the material to teach key concepts and processes

  - step-by-step technical instructions with illustrative examples for performing specific tasks to teach necessary procedural skills

  - animated/video demonstrations of tasks and processes to help learners translate and apply what they learn to real world situations

  - a set of test questions to evaluate comprehension

- a hands-on exercise, served by the Forensic Lab Environment, Alcuin's virtualization component, which includes:
    - a virtual network
    - an automated monitoring and assessment package

Summary

Alcuin's incorporation of multiple learning strategies improves skill acquisition and retention and greatly advances the state of the art in e-learning solutions. Alcuin's online availability and automated evaluation capabilities allows for anytime, anywhere training, greatly reducing training costs and instructor workload. As of December 2010, there is no comparable solution available at any price. The market for cyber training is rapidly expanding in all sectors due to the inability to maintain a sufficiently large, qualified work force capable of responding to the increasing rates of cyber attack.

References

1. Casey, Eoghan (2004a). "Digital Evidence and Computer Crime, Second Edition." Academic Press, San Diego, CA, 2004.

2. Casey, E and Stanley, A. (2004b). "Tool review remote forensic preservation and examination tools." Digital Investigation, Volume 1, Issue 4, doi:10.1016/j.diin.2004.11.003.

3. Watson, I (1997). "Applying Case-Based Reasoning." SF: Morgan Kaufmann Publishers, Inc.

4. Vygotsky, L.S. (1978). "Mind and society: The development of higher mental processes." Cambridge, MA: Harvard University Press, 1978.

5. Collins, A., J. S. Brown, and S. E. Newman (1989). "Cognitive Apprenticeship: Teaching the Crafts of Reading Writing and Mathematics." In L. B. Resnick (Ed.), Knowing, learning, and instruction: Essays in honor of Robert Glaser, ed. L. Resnick, 140-185. Hillsdale, NJ: Lawrence Erlbaum Associates, 1989.

PART III

Appendixes

Historically Significant Case Studies

In Appendices A through E we present historically significant case studies. Although the studies were made prior to 1983, they serve as illuminating examples of the process of developing requirements. Each case study entails important points about "lessons learned."

APPENDIX A

Functional-Requirements Analysis for a Large User Group

Historical Significance

The historical importance of the requirement study described in this Appendix is that it is the best example, of which we are aware, of the selection and characterization process for generating functional requirements of a system to meet the needs of a large user group. It is comprehensive and complete in its description of the user functions.

Current applicability of this Appendix is for designers of systems that need to work for a large user base, for example, a designer trying to determine what functions to include in a SOA-based enterprise architecture. This case study is also applicable to designers of real time systems or complex processor systems such as used in advanced process control systems and/or the telecommunications industry.

An Example Requirement Study

During the rapid growth of the computer industry, little publicity has been given to requirements and requirements-oriented design. Very little has been published in the way of requirements studies.

Furthermore, the proprietary, unpublished requirement studies that have been done tend to be specialized in certain areas. Here we will present an exemplary requirement study that discusses the functional requirements of a large group of users.

This example will begin with the problem definition, which is taken from the Advanced Multiplatform Navy Computer Systems Project (AMNCS). The specific project objectives were to: (1) identify a set of common functions for tactical data systems, (2) identify major common subfunctions for the functions identified, and (3) identify computational functions for the subfunctions. Further objectives of the AMNCS project dealt with computer architecture and technology projection, but they are not discussed here.

Common Functions

In the process of identifying a set of common functions for tactical data systems, two specific groups of functions were identified:

(1) functions that all tactical data systems tended to perform and

(2) specific mission capabilities required of tactical data systems.

Typical functions performed by all tactical data systems are:

(1) data collection

(2) data measurement

(3) data processing

(4) data correlation

(5) data display, and

(6) system executive control.

The following mission-application functions are typically contained in most tactical data systems:

(1) track management

(2) air-interception computations

(3) air-traffic-control computations

(4) strike control computations

(5) electronic warfare

(6) weapons allocation and fire control, etc.

Therefore, when analyzing a particular tactical data system, we may analyze or specify a particular system in terms of its general common functions that exist in all tactical data systems, and its specific mission-oriented functions.

Thus the main difference between tactical data systems in this limited kind of environment will be in the functions included in the concept; the rates of computation of the various kinds of functions; the complexity associated with the computations—decision requirements, number of variable requirements and so on—and the distribution of the functions in the computing system. The system concepts of the tactical data system can cause these changes in requirements on a specific function basis as a result of factors such as degree of computation accuracy, amount of input data, type of computers to be employed in the system, volume and type of communications, physical dynamics of the physical systems, and types of display information that must be generated. After reviewing the list of common and mission-type functions, Shen [1] generated a list of major functions for tactical data systems. We will be interested only in a subset of the major functions and a subset of tactical data systems. Thus, we will define a couple of very small systems here. Table A-1 lists representative U.S. Navy tactical data systems.

Military Branch	Acronym	System Title
Navy	NTDS	Navy Tactical Data System
	ATDS	Air Tactical Data System
	IFDS/FFDS	Integrated Flagship Data System
	MPDS	Message Processing and Distribution System
	ASWSCCS	ASW Ship Command Control System
	ASWCCCS	ASW Centers Command Control System
	OSIS	Ocean Surveillance Intelligence System
	NIPS	Naval Intelligence Processing System
	AEGIS	Advanced Ship Missile System
	IOS/IOIC	Integrated Operational Intelligence System
	JIFDATS	Joint Service Inflight Data Transmission System
	ANEW(VP&VS)	Advanced Airborne ASW System
	STICS/AIDS	Scientific and Technical Center/Airborne Intelligence Data System
	FCSC	Fleet Command Support Center
	Project 749	Ocean Surveillance
	Harpy	(CLASSIFIED)
	TFCC	Tactical Flag Support Center
	LDMX	Local Data Message Exchange
	MTDS	Marine Tactical Data System
Marine Corps	MTACCS	Marine Tactical Command Control System
	TWAES	Tactical Warfare Analysis and Evaluation System
	DTAS	Digital Transmission and Switching System
	TIPI DC/SR	Tactical Information Processing and Interpretation Display, Control, Storage and Retrieval
Joint Services	ASIS/QUEST	Amphibious Support Information System

Table A-1: Representative USN/USMC Systems

Table A-2 lists major functions that appear in the tactical data systems listed in Table A-1, and indicates the various tactical data systems in which the major functions appear.

Shen's report includes twenty-four different kinds of systems from the Navy, the Marine Corps, and the Joint Services. Table A-2 lists major functions and tabulates all twenty-four systems against all major functions.

Table A-1 and Table A-2 are representative of the type of tabulation we would do in a requirements-analysis study. First we list the major functions, both common and mission functions. Next we list the major systems that we would like to analyze or to construct. Then, from the major functions, we list a specific set of functions that are common to the systems that we would like to derive. Finally, we construct a table showing the use of these common functional modules in the various systems.

ASIS	TIPI	DTAS	TWAES	MTACCS	JIFDATS	MTDS	LDMX	TFCC	Harpy	Project 749	FCSC	STICS/AIDS	ANEW	IOS/IOIC	AEGIS	NIPS	OSIS	ASWCCCS	ASWSCCS	MPDS	IFDS/FFDS	ATDS	NTDS	
				×		×				×	×	×	×		×		×		×			×	×	Tracking
				×	×	×		×	×	×	×	×	×	×	×				×			×	×	Sensor Data Process.
	×									×	×	×			×		×	×	×			×	×	Multisensor Corr.
					×					×			×		×							×	×	Sensor Equ. Control
							×	×					×		×				×			×	×	Navigation
													×		×							×		Guidance
				×															×			×	×	Air Traffic Control
				×		×									×							×	×	Air Intercept Control
				×							×		×										×	Terminal Control
				×		×					×				×							×	×	AAW
				×		×					×	×			×							×	×	Strike operations
											×		×									×		AEW
×	×		×	×	×	×	×	×	×	×	×		×	×	×	×	×	×	×			×	×	Data Link Comm.
×	×	×			×		×	×	×	×	×					×	×	×		×	×			Message Process.
×	×	×					×	×	×	×	×						×	×		×	×			Message Dist.
×	×	×	×				×	×	×	×			×		×	×	×	×	×			×	×	Multicomm Control
×	×		×	×	×	×	×	×	×	×	×		×			×	×	×		×		×	×	Secure Comm
×	×		×	×			×	×	×	×	×		×	×	×	×	×	×			×	×		Secure Processing
			×	×		×					×		×		×				×			×	×	Weapon Assignment
×		×	×	×							×	×		×	×		×	×				×	×	Threat Evaluation
			×										×		×									Weapons/Sys/Veh. Sim
×									×		×	×	×	×	×							×	×	EW
									×				×		×							×	×	ECM/ECCM
×					×			×			×		×		×									ELINT
												×	×	×			×	×	×				×	ASW
									×				×									×		Auto Preflight Sys.
×	×	×	×	×			×	×				×	×	×		×	×	×		×	×		×	ISR
×	×	×	×	×		×	×	×			×	×	×	×	×	×	×	×	×	×	×	×	×	Console/CRT Display
				×		×		×			×		×		×		×	×			×	×	×	Geo Display
×	×	×	×			×	×	×			×	×	×		×		×	×	×			×	×	Monitoring
×	×	×	×			×	×	×				×	×		×	×	×	×	×	×	×	×	×	Alert Generation
×	×	×	×			×	×	×				×	×		×	×	×	×	×	×	×	×		Hardware Fault Det.
×												×	×		×		×						×	Software Fault Det.
×		×	×		×		×					×	×		×		×	×					×	Degraded Operations
×	×	×	×			×	×	×				×			×	×	×	×	×	×		×	×	Recovery
×	×		×			×	×					×			×	×	×	×	×			×		Diagnostics
	×	×					×		×			×			×		×					×		Built-in Test
×													×		×			×			×		×	Logistics
×	×			×									×		×			×	×		×	×		Resource Management
×		×	×	×																				Amphibious Warfare
×	×	×	×	×			×	×			×	×	×	×	×		×	×	×			×	×	Data Base Management

Table A-2: System versus Major Functions

This analysis gives us a global definition of the tactical data-system problem in terms of both its common-characteristic functions and its mission-application functions. The result is a complete list of all systems that we intend to utilize, a complete list of all functions that are available to build the systems, and a chart that lists all the systems in connection with the major functions. From this last chart we can determine all the functions that must be computed for any given system. Each system, however, has potentially different requirements, input data rates, and so on. Based on these data rates and the breakout in terms of major functions, we are able to obtain an estimate of the computational complexity of any given system. That is, with rate information we now have the global description of any given system in terms of its system functions. Using the system functions, we will continue to refine each of the functions until we are able to determine the exact computation rates to be used in the synthesis of a computer system. Therefore, our next step will be to take each of the functions—for example, tracking—and break it down into subfunctions. In doing this for the AMNCS Study, Shen breaks the major functions down into a set of seventy-two specific computational requirements (Table A-3). In Shen's study, he tabulates the entire set of seventy-two computational requirements against the set of major functions.

Sensor data preprocessing, which includes parity check, conversion, acceptance, detection, and error correction	Terminal A/C control
S,H xy-speed and heading to rectangular-velocity component conversion (and inverse)	Coordinate conversion or transformation
Data decrypting	R,O xy conversion: range and bearing to rectangular conversion (and inverse)
Track detection	Output formatting
Track Prediction	Report generation
Statistical data combination	Data encrypting

Signal cross-correlation	Communications monitoring
Linear regression analysis	Track identification
Hypothesis testing	Track correlation
Matrix operations	Signal autocorrelation
On-line computational function generations	Statistical-function generation (mean, mode, range, variance, etc.)
Land-mass display	Vector operations
Plotting	Trigonometric functions
Display retrieval	CRT display
A/C flight control (self-contained)	Geographic or vector display
Position fixing	Symbol generation
Platform maintenance	Weapon guidance
Sensor calibration	Ground-based flight control
Triangulation and trilateration	Dead reckoning (S,H xy conversion for position keeping)
Vehicle simulation	Weapon calibration
Automatic frequency allocation and frequency hopping	Weapon simulation
Collision avoidance	Automatic jamming
Platform stabilization and torque	Program compilation
Targeting	Dupe checking
Threat determination	File maintenance
Automatic security checking	Static files
File queries	Data Management
Dynamic files	Complex computational query
IRS index maintenance	Track data smoothing/filtering, which includes adaptive, sliding arc, and growing filtering
Glossary maintenance/retrieval	Signal monitoring
Fast Fourier transform	IFF and SIF processing
Pulse separation	Detection of episodic variations

Power spectral analysis	Audit trail and record keeping
Signal recovery	Message routing
Deghosting	Spooling
Gate testing	
Peripheral device handling	

Table A-3: Computational Requirements for Major Functions

For thirty of the computation requirements from Table A-3, we can generate Table A-4, a chart comparing the computational requirements to the major functions. In this table, for each computational requirement, requirements associated with major functions are designated by X and requirements associated with minor functions are designated with an 0. This further allows detailed definition of typical rates for the functions, functions interaction, parameters that must be passed between the functions, difficult computations, and so on. This level of detail gives an idea of the type of computation rates that must be performed in developing a particular architecture. We still have no information other than rate information that would tend to help us understand the type of detailed computations to be performed. The subfunctions, we have determined, tend to be very small—for example, coordinate-conversion functions. At this level of complexity we are able to break these functions down even further in terms of the system model. Further, having the subfunctions, we can break out and construct a model of any given system. We can start with a tactical data system and construct a figure that, on the left side, consists of a set of all the sensors available, a set of all the functions included in the system, and a set of the outputs in the system.

Using such diagrams, we would be able to break down further the parameters to be passed between subsystems. Each function or subfunction may now be described in terms of its given inputs into the function, computations to be performed, outputs to be returned, and special comments. For example, coordinate conversion, as a function, has a given range and bearing. It computes the x,y coordinates based on the equations $x = rCOS\phi$ $y = rSIN\phi$ and returns as outputs x and y. It may be necessary to extend this function to three dimensions, and this can be noted as a comment. Now we can develop a good description of all functions that must be computed in the system. The diagram specifies all of the parameters and I/O data that must be passed between functions of a particular system.

	Comp. Req.	Sensor Data Preproc.	Coord. Conversion	R. Conversion	S. H Conversion	Output Formatting	Report Generation	Data Encrypting	Data Decrypting	Comm. Monitoring	Track Detection	Track Ident.	Track Prediction	Track Correlation	Statistical Data	Signal Auto. Corr.	Signal Cross Corr.	Statistical Funct.	Linear Regression	Hypothesis	Vector Operation	Matrix Operations	Trig Functions	Comp. Function Gen.	CRT display	Land Mass Display	Geo/Vector	Plotting	Symbol Gen.	Weapons Guidance
Tracking	X		X		0						X	X	X	X	0			0	0	0		X	0	X	0	0	0		X	X
Sensor Data Proc.	X	0	0	0	0			0		0	0	0	0	0	0	0	0	0	0	0	0	0	0	X	0	0	0	0	X	X
Multisensor Corr.	X	X	0		0			0		0	X	X	X		0	X	0	X	0	0	X	0	X	0	X	0	0	0	X	
Sensor Equ. Control	X			0	X										0				0		0			0	0					X
Navigation	X	0	0	X	X			0				X		X	0		0			0	0	0	X	X						X
Guidance	X	0	0	0	0																0	0	X	0						X
Air-Traffic Control	X		0	0	X							X			0			0		X	0	0	X	0	0		0		0	
Air Intercept	0			X						X	X	X	X	0			0		0	X	0	0	X	0			X		X	
Terminal Control	X	X	0		X						X	X	X		0			0	0	X	0	0	X	X	0		X		0	
AAW	X	X	X	X	X	0	0	0	X	X	X	X	X	X	0	0	X	X	X	0	0	X	X	X	X	0	X	X	
Strike Operations	X	X	X		X			X	X	X	X	X	X	0			0	0	X	0	X	0	X	0	X	0	X	X	
AEW	X	X	X	0	X	0	0	0	X	X	X	X	X	0		X	0	X	0	0	X	0	X	0	0		X	X	
Data Link Comm.	X			X	X	0	0	X																						
Message Processing			X	X	0	0	X						0			0			0	0	0	0	0	X	0	0	0	0		
Message Distr.	0		X	X	0	0	X						0			0					0	0								
Multicomm Control			X	X	0	0	X																							
Secure Comm.			0	0	X	X	X																							
Secure Processing			X	X																									0	
Weapons Assignment	X	X	X	0	X	X				X	X	X	X	0			X	0	X	0	0	X	X	X	0	0		X	
Threat Evaluation	X	0	0		X	0				X	X	X	X	0			0	0	X	0	0	X	X	0	X	0	X	X	
Weapons/Sys/Veh Sim				X	0															X	0	X	0	0	0	0	0			
EW	X		0		0					X	X		X	X	0	0	0		0			0	0			0			X
ECM/ECCM	X		0		0								0	0	0	0		0			0	0							X
ELINT	X	0	0			0				X	X		X	X	0	0	X	0	X			X	0		0	0	0	0	
ASW	X	X	X	0	X	0	0	0	X	X	X	X	X	X	0	0	X	0	X	0	X	0	X	X	X	0	0	X	X
Auto Preflight Sys	X				0										0	0		0	X		0								
ISR				X	X	0	0								0									0	X	0	0	0	0	
Database Mgmt	0	0			0		0	0	0					0				0		0			0	0						
Console/CRT Display				X	X	0	0												0						X					X
Geo Display		0	0	0	X	0	0	0						0				0					0		X	X	0	X		X
Monitoring	X									X	X	0	0	0			0	0	0			0	0	X			0	X	
Alert Generation	X			X	0			X	X	X	X	X	X			X	0	X			0	X				X	
Hardware Fault Det				X	X			X																X					
Software Fault Det				X	X																			X					
Degraded Operations																													
Recovery																													
Diagnostics																													
Built-in Test Equip																													
Logistics																													
Resource Management																													

Table A-4: Major Tactical Data-System Functions versus Computational Requirements Partial Table

Conclusion

There is a great deal to be done in requirements analysis. In the previous example the reader will find the partial table of the system versus major functions, a partial list of the subfunctions and their computational requirements for the major functions, and a tabular description of the major tactical data system functions versus the computational required subfunctions. Shen's study is extremely comprehensive at the function, subfunction, and system definition levels; yet it does not go down to the detailed computation rates. This would entail an extraordinary amount of work on a set of systems as complex as found in the total navy application spectrum. There are, however, studies that take limited system concepts down to detailed levels. An example of such a specific-system analysis is given in the next chapter.

Reference

1. Shen, J.P. "Advanced Multiplatform Navy Computer Systems (AMNCS)." NELC/TR1847 (September 1972).

APPENDIX B

Requirements Analysis of a Single Application

Historical Significance

The historical importance of the requirement study described in this Appendix is that it is the best example, of which we are aware, of the selection and characterization process designed to select a processor to perform a specific set of well defined functions. The process illustrated and included in this appendix describes the detail required for a specific real time platform.

Current applicability of this Appendix is for designers of real time systems. Such systems are used in advanced process control systems and/or the telecommunications industry. There are a number of manufacturers of chip sets in the embedded processing area whose products can be used in this type of a system, but you would have to do a detailed study to determine the particular support chips to use with the processor to provide your desired functionality. Further, this study would be useful if you were going to develop support chips for the systems provided by embedded processor manufacturers, develop FPGLAs, or gate array systems. Lastly, if you were developing board-based systems this study would help you decide on the features to put in your board-based system.

Kilpatrick's Air-to-Ground Attack-Aircraft Requirements Analysis

Kilpatrick [1] considered detailed requirements for a number of specific systems. One such system is comparable to one of the smallest of the twenty or so systems considered by Shen in Appendix A. In particular, we consider the air-to-ground attack-system concept and review the system functional description in detail. A summary of the concept is given in Figure B-l. It consists of electro-optical functions for target acquisition, a threat-warning function, a fire-control function, three variations of navigation functions, an air-data function, a flight-control function, a digital-data-link function, and a display function. These functions are all sensor-processing functions that connect into a system via various types of I/O links. The system concept was a distributive processor memory system and is therefore listed as a DPM (distributed processor/ memory) processor. DPM does the appropriate computations on the data and performs the appropriate functions associated with the functional concepts displayed in Figure B-l.

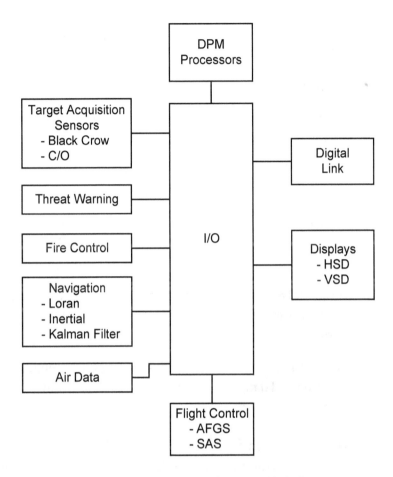

Figure B-1: Air-to-ground attack-concept block diagram

The primary subfunctions provided by the system are:

- Black Crow: a particular method of target detection

- Electro-optic: a particular means of target recognition used by the Air Force

- EW/ECM: the electronic-warfare, electronic-countermeasures function used for threat-warning location and neutralization of enemy vehicles.

- FLR: a forward-looking radar function, which is used for target acquisition, the navigation function, and weapon delivery.

- Loran/inertial: part of the navigation function.

- Flight Control: the stability-augmentation function (SAF) and the attitude flight-control system function (AFCS).

- Digital Link: a function that provides two-way communication between the aircraft and the ground.

- Vertical-Situation Display: a function that gives a pilot flight-direction, sensor-imagery, and weapon-delivery information.

- Horizontal Situation Display: a function that provides navigation information, threat and target location, and sensory-image functions to the pilot.

- Control Unit/Data Entry: provides for subsystem mode of operation and data insertion into the computer from the pilot.

From the subfunction definitions and detailed equations and the block diagram that shows the interaction of all the functions, the requirements analysis is begun. Kilpatrick first generates the I/O data-transfer requirements. There are some important points to be noted about these requirements. The system block diagram of Figure B-1 can provide a listing of all primary information that must be transferred within the machine and processed within the system. Each subsystem shown on the block diagram has a number of other functions associated with it. These are preflight functions: on-off power test and various kind of status signals that do not affect the I/O with a memory of the actual system itself. Note that we see none of this preflight type information in the operational requirements. Because of lack of information on some functions, assumptions may have to be made. Typical assumptions are as follows:

To determine the rate for the system-monitoring sensors, the assumption is made that thirty different sensors or test points will be sampled ten times per second. Typical parameters to be tested include fuel quantity, fuel flow, engine revolutions per minute (RPM), oil pressure, and so on.

To obtain a rate for the digital data link, it is assumed that the outputs from the link are coupled into the autopilot during automatic landings and that the message rates do not exceed one per second.

Data rates for displays are determined by the refresh rate and the number of signals being displayed. In Kilpatrick's analysis, it is assumed that fifty symbols will be required on the horizontal-situation display and that the symbol position is not updated at a rate to exceed ten times per second. The symbols that are displayed are assumed to be representative of targets, threats, range marks, and the like. It is assumed that the display is refreshed at either ten or sixty times per second from the memory. Further, it is assumed that if the display is refreshed directly from the main system memory, the I/O rate per word is sixty times per second. Otherwise, if the display has its own private buffer memory, the I/O rate only occurs ten times per second.

Detailed Functional Analysis

With the information about the I/O and now the information detailing the interaction of data between the various functions, the requirements-definition process proceeds by breaking each separate functions into a detailed analysis of its algorithm and other parameters. For the air-to-ground attack aircraft, we will take one such function and discuss it in detail. Again, this function is taken from Kilpatrick. The purpose of this function, particularly concerning digital flight control, is to show the depth to which we must go into the computations. After discussing the digital-flight-control process in detail, we summarize the total system requirements that we could develop for every function in the same detail. Following this requirement analysis, we can derive a machine that meets the requirements or at least the performance requirements of the computational requirements for the air-to-ground control environment. We have picked digital flight control because most readers are familiar with the types of equations involved for the flight-control function.

Kilpatrick has developed a representation of a pre-access digital flight-control system. The system offers stability augmentation of the platform on every axis and other loop modes of altitude hold, mach hold, pitch hold, automatic landing, and heading hold. Heading hold provides control of the aircraft's lateral flight in response to a variety of steering functions. This flight-control system includes automatic operation of the outer loops with pilot override and adjustment capabilities. The pilot and flight director have the capability of closing the outer loops. From such analysis the main computations are summarized.

The main driving computation in the flight-control function consists of a number of digital filters that are used to smooth and filter input data. Notably, these functions are difficult to compute. For the type of system being considered by Kilpatrick, the coefficients, since they take a limited range of values, are precomputed and stored as constants. A memory-instruction cycle-time estimate for the computation of the digital filters must be prepared and tabulated. These are the number of digital filters required in the particular flight-control system used in the air-to-ground attack mission. Note that the instructions are categorized as either M (for multiply or divide) or O for other types of instructions). The M instruction is typically a long instruction, and the O instruction is typically a single-word instruction requiring only a few memory cycles. Instruction-count estimates that estimate the number of instructions, the frequency, and the integration rate—thereby giving us the total number of instructions necessary to implement the digital-filter portion of the flight-control systems—can be developed. For each function, the following information must be provided:

(1) the number of instructions of both the multiply and other category necessary to implement the function; (2) the number of times that a particular function appears within a group in the actual digital-filter algorithm; (3) the number of times the functions must be computed; and (4) utilizing the instructions, the frequency, and the iteration rate, the total number of instructions to be executed per unit time or per second. Taking the number of roll, pitch, and yaw accesses. understanding that the I/O must yet be implemented and assuming that all pitch outer-loop modes can be performed simultaneously—the total number of instructions for digital flight control can be computed. Some assumptions may be required, however. We must assume that the flight-control and stability-augmentation loop iterations are eighty per second for pitch and yaw and forty per second for roll, and twenty per second for pitch and roll outer loops. There are a number of other functions involved that would require computational time. These include signal median select, control gain compensation and gain scheduling, executive overhead, built-in test equipment and built-in test-analysis overhead, mode switching, and the effect of computing redundant channels of the stability-augmentation function to ensure that the vehicle does not crash because of a failure in this subsystem. These functions may take a significant amount of time, particularly compared with the digital filters and I/O. In a vehicle the digital filters and I/O typically require about 38 percent of the processing time. The median-select function requires about 24 percent. Control gain and gain scheduling require about 18 percent. The executive-overhead, test-equipment, and mode-switching functions require about 20 percent. Redundant computations then require that the digital filter and I/O function be duplicated in separate processes so that they may occur simultaneously. Kilpatrick determines the functional breakdown by percentage from a heavy-lift helicopter analysis that actually computed all the functions. Kilpatrick summarizes the total functions for the digital flight-control system by scaling up the computations for the digital filter and I/O function by the percentage given from the heavy-lift helicopter-analysis study.

Furthermore, the input/output—since input/output in most systems tends to be customized—is not an exact function. However, Kilpatrick is able to specify the variables and the frequency per second at which the functions of the autopilot/flight director are transmitted. Thus a set of processing requirements can be developed and summarized for each function. By summing the functions, the total system can be described.

Total Computation Requirements

We have discussed only one of the functions and that only in limited detail. Table B-1 indicates the functions and memory cycles in thousands per second for the complete air-to-ground attack system shown in Figure B-l. Since Kilpatrick makes the assumption of essentially a single-address machine with two memory cycles required for the execution of such simple instructions as load or add, a total computer memory cycle or instruction rate can be determined.

Function	Memory Cycles (thousands/second)
LORAN	150
Inertial (SD/PLAT)	400/50
Air data	30
Flight control/channel	350
Flight control	350
Kalman filter	100
Display	200
Black Crow	300
Total: Air-to-ground attack concept (maximum). *Note: Black Crow and fire-control functions are assumed not to be performed at the same time.*	1,600/1,250

Table B-1: Air-to-Ground Attack-Concept Processor-Speed-Requirements Summary

On the basis of all this analysis, the memory requirements for the air-to-ground attack concept are given in Table B-2 and the I/O requirements in Table B-3. The I/O requirements, memory requirements, and system-cycle speeds, along with the detailed block diagrams and detailed functional block diagrams, complete the requirements analysis for this one function. Therefore, we can begin the synthesis of the actual computing system involved with this function.

One further issue that we must consider is not specifically brought out in Kilpatrick's requirements study. That issue is phasing. For example, in many military systems and even in commercial systems, not all the defined functions are or must be performed at the same time. For example, in a university computing-center environment, the system may always be available for batch processing and may also run a time-share foreground program between 7:00 a.m. and 7:00 p.m. Thus the processing of the university computing center could be divided into two phases: one phase from 7:00 p.m. to 7:00 a.m., consisting solely of batch processing, and a second phase consisting of both batch and time-share processing. In Kilpatrick's study the system was being sized for the maximum load, which is the computation of all those functions shown in the block diagram in Figure B-1.

Function	Memory Words (Instruction Data)	
LORAN	3,900	500
Inertial	2,200	350
Air data	1,300	70
Flight control	3,250	400
Kalman filter	800	2,000
Fire control	4,800	500
Display	2,500	500
Black Crow	1,500	2,500
Total: Air-to-ground attack concept	20,250	6,800

Table B-2: Air-to-Ground Attack-Concept Memory-Requirements Summary

System	Data Words/Second Inputs	Outputs
LORAN	50	75
Inertial (SD/PLAT)	600/150	30
Air data	50	—
Flight control	600	200
Fire control	—	—
Kalman filter	—	—
Radar altimeter	20	—
Radar	20	40
E/O	40	40
Display	—	1,000/4,000
Link	10	10
Black Crow	1,000	—
Total	2,400/2,000	1,400/4,400

Table B-3: Air-to-Ground Attack I/O Requirements Summary

Conclusion

Detailed decomposition of an actual system and its functions is a difficult and tedious process, as has been illustrated. Attention paid to detail early in the system design, however, more than repays the initial efforts if the system requirements ever change.

Reference

1. Kilpatrick, P.S. All Semiconductor Distributed Aerospace Processors/ Memory Study, Volume 1: Avionics Processing Requirements, August 1973, Technical Report AFAL-TER-72-226.

APPENDIX C

Generating Requirements for General-Purpose Systems

Historical Significance

The historical importance of the requirement study described in this Appendix, is that it is the best example, of which we are aware, of the selection and characterization process designed to select a processor based upon functional characteristics. The processors included in this study are pioneering examples of capabilities that we currently take for granted.

Current applicability of this Appendix is for designers of real time systems or single processor systems such as those used in advanced process control systems, PDAs, and/or the telecommunications industry. There are a number of manufacturers of chip sets in the embedded processing area whose products could be used in this type of a system, but you would have to do a detailed study to determine the support chips to use with the processor to provide your desired functionality. Further, this study would be useful if you were going to develop support chips for the systems provided by embedded processor manufacturers, develop FPGLAs, or gate array systems. Lastly, if you were developing board-based systems this study would help you decide on the features to put in your board-based system.

This requirements study took place between 1964 and 1978.

Examples of Requirement Studies for General-Purpose Computers

For general-purpose data-processing systems, the functional requirements cannot always be well defined. Further, very little detailed information exists about requirement studies for general-purpose computer systems.

There is a reason for the lack of visible detailed requirements studies of general-purpose business applications. For example, the data-processing industry has grown so rapidly and the demand for machines has been so high—and the sophistication of the user simultaneously so low—that the user has not demanded the sort of detailed analysis of his problems and requirements that has been done in the military environment. Further, the competitive nature of the industry has kept any analysis that has been done proprietary. In the military environment there are environmental and other restrictions that necessitate detailed analysis of the systems, whereas in the civilian data-processing environment the principal requirement to date has been for upward software compatibility to ensure that the user's application programs will run on any new equipment he may purchase from a manufacturer. As the data-processing industry matures, however, more and more detailed requirements analysis will be done. A glaring example of the lack of systems requirements analysis in the civilian environment was that of the fiasco with airline reservation systems, in which double-bookings occurred due to the lack of process synchronization. Superficially, there appeared to be plenty of machines and multiprocessors that could be hooked together to provide enough throughput rate. Yet because the detailed functional analysis requirement, I/O interaction, functional interaction, subfunction interaction, and module definition of the functions were not accomplished, these machines, though theoretically able to solve the problem, were ineffective.

This is not to imply, however, that detailed requirements analysis will solve the computing-synthesis problem. Many military systems that have been analyzed extensively fail to perform adequately—or at all. The solution to computer-system synthesis problems is careful synthesis and design based on requirements but employing good engineering judgment. Although few general-purpose computing-system requirement studies have been performed or discussed in the literature, there are two classic examples of such studies. One of these was done for the IBM 360 series [1] the other for the DEC PDP-11 computer [2]. Both of these articles contain general descriptions of the design objectives, the major architectural decisions, and some of the reasons for those architectural decisions. In the requirement study done for the IBM 360, much analysis of the type described in Appendix A has been done either by IBM or by the customer. Since the machine to be designed is general purpose, the data from the detailed requirement studies have been analyzed, resulting in a series of design goals for the new computer system. Since both the PDP-11 and the IBM 360 are general-purpose machines, the user base is very large; thus we are not able to analyze the detailed needs of any given customer. It is hoped that in designing such machines, we will be able to generalize the requirements of the users in such a way that we can meet the needs of a broad market segment.

The reason that these two summaries of requirement studies are so important is that the IBM 360 and the PDP-11 are both very successful commercial machines. Therefore, although the requirement studies may appear superficial, the implications of the information bases from which these requirements were derived is significant in that the designers were able to interpret correctly the requirements of their user base—hence the commercial success of these machines.

IBM System 360 Requirement Study

There were four major innovations in the IBM System 360:

1.   A flexible storage concept that provided variable capacity, a hierarchy of different speed memories, storage protection, and program relocation.

2. An I/O system that provided concurrent operation, large amounts of channel capacity, an integrated design between the hardware and software and CPU interaction, and a standard channel interface.

3. A general-purpose machine organization with very powerful operating system, logical processing operations, and many different instruction and data formats.

4. Machine-level language compatibility over a series of models with a performance range of over 50.

In developing the architecture of the IBM 360, several important systems concepts and trends were noted by Amdahl et al [1]. These are:

1. The adaption of business data processing to scientific data-processing equipment.

2. The total-system concept, including I/O.

3. The use of program translators.

4. The development of large secondary-storage mechanisms such as tapes, drums, and discs with many-order-of-magnitude larger storage capabilities than seen in previous media.

5. Real-time and time-sharing system development.

On the basis of these general technical trends, a number of different concepts were provided for in the 360 system. Some of these design objectives or requirements are described in this section.

The major requirements for the system can be grouped into five areas:

1. Provide for advanced system concepts.

2. Provide an open-ended design.

3. Ensure a general-purpose functional capability.

4.   Provide a cost-effective performance range.

5.   Produce complete intermodule software compatibility.

Each of these five requirements includes a number of subrequirements. We shall review these five major areas and discuss in general or list the major subrequirements of each.

In the advanced-concept area it was recognized that a major break would have to be made with existing products even though this would result in some software incompatibility. The break would establish the new family of machines. Therefore, the following subrequirements of the advanced-concept requirement were considered:

1.   That the computer allow for a family capability to provide growth and to allow for a succession of product lines.

2.   That a high-performance general I/O technique be developed that would allow I/O devices tailored for application to be used with any machines, even though the I/O devices differed in rate, access times, or functionality (also, that the input/output control programs had to be designed to be compatible with each other).

3.   To develop an information system that utilizes the throughput of a machine to obtain high-speed problem solution by making a complex machine and programming system that are easy for the user to manipulate.

4.   To increase central processing unit (CPU) utilization for computing by providing for additional compilation, I/O management, and so on.

5.   To provide a comprehensive operating system that includes extensive interrupt facilities and good storage protection.

6.   To provide a failsafe/failsoft capability in systems with more than one CPU.

7. To provide a large storage capability rather than the 32,000 words normally required and furnished at that time.

8. To provide for large word lengths to accommodate large fixed and floating point words.

9. To provide detailed hardware maintenance and diagnostic aids to reduce system downtime and make identification of individual malfunctions easier.

The open-ended design requirement was an attempt to assure customers that when they made the break with previous software concepts, they would have a long-term viable computer system that would continue to use the same architecture but could be upgraded for speed and performance over a long period of time. This enabled IBM to satisfy its customers that when they made the switch to the new machine, they would not have to make another switch in three or four years.

A number of subrequirements were identified in this area. These are:

1. That the new design had to provide customer programming capability for over a decade; thus the machines would have to continue to use the same architecture for at least a decade.

2. That the design permit asynchronous operation of major subsystems so that subsystems could be updated without affecting the total system configuration.

3. That many decisions be made to ensure that the functions of the machine would be general—that is, that spare bits and the like be carefully placed in the words to ensure that new techniques or new functions that came along did not make the new product line obsolete.

4. That hardware and software control be embodied in the machine in such a way that it could directly sense control

and respond to other equipment modules by means of techniques that are outside the normal techniques. This would provide for the construction of supersystems that could be dynamically managed from the basic system, which would allow for the construction of special systems designed for specific applications and for the construction of systems wherein some short-sightedness in the original design had been encountered.

In order to meet varying requirements such as those found in commercial, scientific, time-sharing, data reduction, communications, and other types of processing, the 360 CPU would have to be capable of hosting three different applications. Thus different types of facilities might have to be offered as options but would have to appear as integral features from the viewpoint of the system's logical structure. In particular, the general-purpose objective dictated:

1. That manipulation of words or bits be such that the operation depends on the general representation rather than on any specific selection of bits.

2. That operations be code independent—that is, that all bit combinations be acceptable as data and no data be permitted to exert any control function on the machine.

3. That bits be addressable.

4. That the addressing structure be able to address directly the unit used for character representation—that is, addressability to the byte.

The main consideration in the performance area is that the various products in the product line have a consistent cost/performance ratio that decreases or remains stable as the system performance increases. There is a large problem in this area, however, because of the compatibility constraint.

The last IBM 360 requirement was for intermodel compatibility. At least six models were anticipated with a performance range of 50.

Intermodel compatible really meant program compatible. Program compatible meant that any valid program whose logic did not depend implicitly on time of execution or other side effects of programming that would run on configuration A would also run on configuration B if B contained at least the required storage, I/O devices, and optional features. A hedge clause was placed in this description such that any invalid program that violated the programmer's manual was not constrained by the manufacturer to yield the same results and thus was not strictly program compatible. Therefore, if the programmer stayed within the specification in the programmer's manual, since the architecture of all the machines was identical, they could run programs on any IBM 360 structure regardless of the speed differences between models. The program could run at different rates, however.

Amdahl et al.[1] describes how some of the previously summarized requirements drove the decisions made for the IBM 360 machine design . In this appendix, however, we are interested only in the requirements and thus will not delve deeper into the IBM 360 architecture. We will, however, make the point that in conducting any type of requirement study—whether a general-purpose one such as is done for the 360 or a detailed special-purpose requirement study such as was done earlier in this Appendix—the design step must begin somewhere. It is difficult to break out of the mode of determining the requirements and start to design. Therefore, it is almost irrelevant where we begin the design except that at some point, we must ask: If we make this selection,how does this affect the other requirements? In the IBM 360, for example, this was accomplished by considering the basic addressing structure and first determining what the data format should be. The first decision was to go with an 8-bit byte. Once this decision is made, the design can proceed. We can lay out the formats and work on the field specifications and the instruction decisions. The system architects can go to work synthesizing the various configurations. The architects will thus know how big the machine will tend to be, what kind of addressing modes are envisioned, how the memories have to be addressed, and so on.

The point is, if during the requirement study we get into a circular mode of thinking, then it is **time to make a decision**! After making that first decision, we can assess the impact on the requirements and, if necessary, change the decision. It is important to begin the design process and cut down the amount of information we are required to deal with in general terms. The specifics we decide on can be traded off against each other so that the system design may progress.

DEC PDP-11 Requirement Study

The PDP-11 requirement study is slightly different from the IBM requirement study. Whereas IBM decided to make a major break from its architectures, the PDP-11 was designed without regard to whether it would represent a major break. Rather, it was designed to solve certain technical problems that had been encountered by customers of the DEC Corporation. DEC is in the minicomputer business. Its customers were using four different machines at the time the PDP-11 was conceived: a PDP-5, a LINC, a PDP-4, and a PDP-8. Further, these models were being used in communication-control environments, in instrumentation environments, as preprocessors and communication processors for large systems, for data acquisitions, and so on. The PDP-11 was designed to overcome weaknesses that had been encountered in the current DEC mini-computers based on the customer's application experience. The weaknesses the PDP-11 was to overcome, included: (1) limited addressing space, (2) too few registers, (3) lack of hardware stack capability, (4) slow context switching among multiple processes, (5) lack of byte-string manipulation capability, (6) lack of read-only-memory storage facilities, (7) elementary I/O concepts, (8) lack of ability to upgrade users to a higher-performance model, and (9) high programming costs as a result of lack of high-level languages and their associated software support. The new machine family was to take advantage of new integrated-circuit technologies that were becoming available; to contain enough machine models to span a range of functions and performance; to update the DEC product lines to what are considered classical third-generation machines; to work equally well in the addressing-mode mechanizations 0-, 1-, or 2-address machine; and to present the user with a very sophisticated connection system that later became known as the Unibus.

Notably, the PDP-11 requirements tended to be much simpler than the IBM 360 requirements. There are a number of reasons for this, including the size of machine, the size of the corporation and its market base, and the context in which the machines were used. One will note, however, that the requirements that were used to define the PDP-11 are very distinct and direct with respect to the changes that must be made to be successful in the minicomputer business.

Conclusion

This appendix has tried to provide a feel for the types of things that have to be done to define a system. There are a number of different ways to look at a general-purpose system's requirements. One way is to see it as a detailed application. This is the way most military systems are viewed. In these cases, the user has complete control over a specific application and may buy either a general-purpose or a custom-designed machine. Because of the time-critical factors and other severe constraints on the machine—such as form factors of space, weight, power, and reliability—the user usually dictates a detailed application to be performed, and machines are very carefully analyzed and designed to fit into one particular environment. In contrast, some requirement studies that might appear superficial actually describe the kind of information distilled from a large customer base, which drives the definition of a large long-range commercial product line. We have shown simple examples of the major requirements that went into the IBM 360 and DEC PDP-11 series. An individual user, in evaluating one of these systems for use in his application, may perform the detailed analysis shown in the military-systems analysis example to ensure that the computer system meets his needs. Experience in developing product-line machines for large general-purpose environments, however, shows that the simple statements appearing in the DEC and the IBM 360 series requirement analysis are more than adequate to begin the development of such machines. Companies such as Univac Defense Systems Division and IBM Federal Systems Division, which have a large base of military customers, are beginning to have the ability to define product lines on the basis of requirement studies on the order of the 360 and PDP-11 requirement studies. This is because of the large customer base. In this environment, however, companies are constrained to keep the architecture functionality the same for all systems and to package the machines in different types of configurations and form factors. Papers by Case and Palays [3] and Strecker [4] describe how the 370 relates to the 360 and how the VAX relates to the PDP, respectively.

References

1. Amdahl, G.M., et al. "Architecture of the IBM System/360." IBM Journal of Research and Development (April 1964): 87-101.

2. Bell, G., et al. "A New Architecture for Mini Computers—the DEC PDP-11." Proceedings of the 1970 Spring Joint Computer Conference, pp. 657-675.

3. Case, R.P., and Palays, A. "Architecture of the IBM System/370." LALM (January 1978): 73-96.

4. Strecker, W.D. "VAX-11/780, A Virtual Address Extension to the DEC PDP-11." Proc. NCL (1978): 967-980.

APPENDIX D

Processor Selection Process

Historical Significance

This requirements study is historically signiciant because it is one of the best examples (if not the best) of the selection process of a processor based upon functional characteristics.

Current applicability of this Appendix is for designers of real time systems or single processor systems such as those used in advanced process control systems, PDAs, and/or the telecommunications industry. There are a number of manufacturers of chip sets in the embedded processing area whose products could be used in this type of a system, but you would have to do a detailed study to determine the support chips to use with the processor to provide your desired functionality.

In this Appendix, we review a well-motivated effort to design a computer architecture to meet a broad profile of data-processing requirements in the 1980-1990 time frame. Two government agencies that employed computers for data processing, research and command, and control and communications set up a joint committee to select a basic computer architecture to serve their needs for at least a decade.

The committee pioneered a new approach to quantifying the relative performance of alternative computer architectures.

Committee members were concerned with selecting a computer architecture suitable for implementation in future military computers, and they wanted to evaluate the merits of architecture independent of any features—or flaws—or existing implementations. The definition of computer architecture used was: the structure of the computer a programmer needs to know in order to write any (timing-independent) machine-language program that will run correctly on the computer. Thus the architectural definition used in the computer family architecture (CFA) studies was essentially that of an instruction-set architecture (ISA).

In the first phase of the activity, the committee screened an initial field of nine candidate architectures using a prefilter consisting of both absolute and quantitative criteria. The selection process was initiated with the following initial set of nine computer architectures:

1. Burroughs 6700

2. DEC PDP-11

3. IBM System/370

4. Interdata 8/32

5. Litton AN/GYK-12

6. Rolm AN/UYK-28

7. SEL 32

8. AN/UYK-7

9. AN/UYK-20

The AN/GYK-12 is a militarized computer widely used by the U.S. Army, whereas the AN/UYK-7 and AN/UYK-20 are standard U.S. Navy shipboard computers. The AN/UYK-28 is a rugged computer that is instruction-set upward-compatible with the Data General Nova computer.

Because of financial and time limitations, the committee limited its first-stage goal to finding three good architectures.

In a second phase, a more rigorous analysis was applied to the three highest-ranking architectures in the first stage. In addition to test programs, these architectures were evaluated on the basis of their existing support software base and life-cycle cost estimates [1,2]. The more intensive, test-program phase of the evaluation gave the same ordering of architectures—Interdata 8/32, DEC PDP-11, and IBM S/370—as the initial rank ordering based on the absolute and quantitative criteria.

Absolute Criteria

The committee specified nine absolute criteria that it felt a candidate computer architecture must satisfy to meet the requirements of future military computer systems. All the absolute criteria (with the exception of subsetability) had to be satisfied by an implementation of the architecture that was already operational. This eliminated speculative decisions based on promises or potential solutions that looked inviting but might not come to fruition. Failure to satisfy any absolute criterion resulted in the elimination of the architecture from further consideration. The definitions of the nine absolute criteria are:

1. Virtual-memory support: The architecture must support a virtual-to-physical translation mechanism.

2. Protection: The architecture must have the capability to add new, experimental (that is, not fully debugged) programs that may include I/O without endangering the reliable operation of existing programs.

3. Floating-point support: The architecture must explicitly support one or more floating point data types with at least one of the format yielding more than ten decimal digits of significance in the mantissa.

4. Interrupts and traps: It must be possible to write a trap handler that is capable of executing a procedure to respond to any trap condition and then resume operation of the program if logically possible. The architecture must also be defined so that it is capable of resuming execution following any interrupt (for example, I/O power failure, disk read error).

5. Subsetability: At least the following components of an architecture must be able to be factored out of the full architecture:

    • Virtual-to-physical address translation mechanism.

    • Floating-point instructions and registers (if separate from general-purpose registers).

    • Decimal-instructions set (if present in full architecture).

    • Protection mechanism.

6. Multiprocessor support: The architecture must allow for multiprocessor configurations. Specifically, it must support some form of test-and-set instruction to allow the implementation of synchronization functions such as P and V.

7. Controllability of I/O: A processor must be able to exercise absolute control over any I/O processor and/or I/O controller.

8. Extendability: The architecture must have some method of adding instructions to the architecture consistent with existing formats. There must be at least one undefined code point in the existing opcode space of the instruction formats.

9. Read-only code: The architecture must allow programs to be kept in a read-only section of primary memory.

Quantitative Criteria

In addition to the absolute criteria, the committee specified quantitative criteria for the initial screening process. A number of these attributes would be better measured by benchmarks or test programs. Lacking the resources to run benchmarks on all nine candidate architectures, the committee used quantitative criteria to select three or four candidate architectures for more intensive study via test programs.

The quantitative criteria are next defined briefly. As with the absolute criteria, complete definitions can be found in the committee's final report [1].

1. Virtual-address space:

    - $V1$: The size of the virtual-address space in bits.

    - $V2$: Number of addressable units in the virtual-address space.

2. Physical-address space:

    - $P1$: The size of the physical-address space in bits.

    - $P2$: The number of addressable units in the physical-address space.

3. Fraction of instruction space unassigned, where ui is the number of unassigned instructions of length i.

4. Size of central processor state:

    - $CS1$: The number of bits in the processor state of the full architecture.

    - $CS2$: The number of bits in the processor state of the minimum subset of the architecture (that is, without floating point, decimal, protection, or address-translation registers).

    - $CM1$: The number of bits that must be transferred between the processor and primary memory to first save the processor state of the full architecture upon interruption and then restore the processor state prior to resumption.

- *CM2*: The measure analogous to CMl for the minimum subset of the architecture.

5. Virtualizability: K is unity if the architecture is virtualizable as defined by Popek and Goldberg [1], otherwise K is zero.

6. Usage base:

- *B1*: Number of computers delivered as of the latest date for which data prior to 1 June 1976.

- *B2*: Total dollar value of the installed computer base as of the latest date for which data exist prior to 1 June 1976.

7. I/O initiation: I is the minimum number of bits that must be transferred between main memory and any processor (central or I/O) in order to output one 8-bit byte to a standard peripheral device.

8. Direct instruction addressability: D is the maximum number of bits of primary memory that one instruction can address directly given a single-base register, which may be used but not modified.

9. Maximum interrupt latency: L is the maximum number of bits that may need to be transferred between memory and any processor (central, I/O, and so on) between the time an interrupt is requested and the time the computer starts processing that interrupt (given that interrupts are enabled).

10. Subroutine linkage:

- *J1*: The number of bits that must be transferred between the processor and the memory to save the user

state, transfer to the called routine, restore the user
state, and return to the calling routine for full
architecture.

- *J2*: The analogous measure to S1 for the minimum
architecture (for example, without floating-point
registers).

Composite Scoring of the Quantitative Criteria

After applying the quantitative criteria, the committee had to
determine how the performance of the candidate architectures
would be used to select three or four for further consideration. The
architectures could be ordered relative to each of the quantitative
criteria and these independent orderings studied to detect weaknesses and strengths of the competing architectures. Some summary
measure would ultimately be needed, however, to assist the
committee in its selection. A variety of thresholding and weighting
schemes were proposed, and the following one was chosen.

Each voting organization represented on the committee was
allowed 100 points to distribute among the various measures to
indicate their relative importance to the organization. The weight
for criterion, $W(x)$ was defined as the total number of points given
criterion by all the voting organizations, divided by the total number
of points handed out. When attempting to combine these quantitative measures into a composite measure, the committee faced two
problems. First, the measures are defined so that good computer
architectures maximize some measures and minimize others. This
problem was resolved by defining a composite measure to be a
maximal measure and transforming all minimal measures to
maximal measures by taking their reciprocals [2].

Second, measures that inherently involve large magnitudes are
not necessarily more important than smaller measures. The values
for the quantitative criteria were normalized by dividing each
value by the average value of the criterion over the set of nine

architectures. Such normalized measures have the attractive properties of lying in the range (0,M), having a mean across the set of M architectures of unity; and having the standard deviation of the set of normalized measures in the interval (0,M). For some measures they took the normalization process further and adjusted the spread so that the measure gave a standard deviation of unity across the set of architectures being evaluated [2]. To combine the individual measures, the committee used a simple, linear sum of each normalized measure X scaled by its corresponding weighting coefficient W(x). The weighting coefficients were defined so that they summed to unity; hence the composite measure A is in fact a normalized measure with a mean of 1. The ranking and scores are shown in Table D-1.

Architecture	Score
Interdata 8/32	1.68
PDP-11	1.43
IBM S/370	1.36
AN/GYK-12	0.94
AN/UYK-28	0.92
B6700	0.91
SEL-32	0.86
AN/UYK-7	0.46
AN/UYK-20	0.44

Table D-1. Architecture Ranking and Composite Score

This ranking, applied with the results of the absolute criteria, reduced the field of candidate architectures to three finalists (the Interdata 8/32, the DEC PDP-11, and the IBM S/370) for more thorough evaluation.

Test-Program Evaluation Process

Many parameters of a computer architecture can be determined directly from its principles-of-operation manual, but the committee felt that the only practical test of its quality would be to evaluate its performance against a set of benchmark or test programs [3]. Throughout the application of the foregoing absolute and quantitative criteria, which were intended primarily as prefiltering techniques, the committee felt that a benchmarking phase would be needed. The committee defined a test program as a relatively small program (100-500 machine instructions) representative of a program class.

Test-Program Specification

The committee considered a number of alternative test-program specifications. The full specification of the twelve selected test programs is given in the final report [1]. A brief description is presented here:

1. I/O kernel, four priority levels, requires the processor to field interrupts from four devices, each of which has its own priority level. While one device is being processed, interrupts from higher-priority devices are allowed.

2. I/O kernel, first in, first out (FIFO) processing, also fields interrupts from four devices but without consideration of priority level. Instead, each interrupt causes a request for processing to be queued; requests are processed in FIFO order. While a request is being processed, interrupts from other devices are allowed.

3. I/O device handler processes application programs' requests for I/O block transfers on a typical tape drive, and returns the status of the transfer upon completion.

4.   Large fast fourier transform (FFT) computes the fast Fourier transform of a large vector of 32-bit floating-point complex numbers. The benchmark exercises the machine's floating-point instructions but principally tests its ability to manage a large address space. (Up to 500,000 bytes may be required for the vector.)

5.   Character search searches a long character string for the first occurrence of a potentially large argument string. It exercises the ability to move through character strings sequentially.

6.   Bit test, set, or reset tests the initial value of a bit within a bit string, then optionally sets or resets the bit.

7.   Runge-Kutta integration numerically integrates a simple differential equation using third-order Runge-Kutta integration. It is primarily a test of floating-point arithmetic and iteration mechanisms.

8.   Linked-list insertion inserts a new entry in a doubly linked list. This is a test of pointer-manipulation capability.

9.   Quicksort sorts a potentially large vector of fixed-length strings using a quicksort algorithm. Like FFT, it tests the ability to manipulate a large address space; but it also tests the ability of the machine to support recursive routines.

10. ASCII to floating point converts an ASCII string to a floating-point number. It exercises character-to-numeric conversion.

11. Boolean matrix transpose transposes a square, tightly packed bit matrix. It tests the ability to sequence through bit vectors by arbitrary increments.

12. Virtual-memory space exchange changes the virtual-memory mapping context of the processor.

Measures of Architectural Performance

Very little has been done in the past to quantify the relative (or absolute) performance of computer architectures independent of specific implementations. The committee defined measures of architecture performance. Computer performance is measured in units of space and time [2]. The measures used by the committee to measure a computer 'architecture's performance on the test programs were:

1. *Measure of space*: S is the number of bytes used to represent a test program.

2. *Measure of execution time*: M is the number of bytes transferred between primary memory and the processor during the execution of the test program.

3. *R* is the number of bytes transferred among internal registers of the processor during execution of the test program.

All the measures described in this section were measured in units of 8-bit bytes. All computer architectures under consideration were based on 8-bit bytes; hence the byte unit of measurement could be conveniently applied to all these machines.

Test Program Size

An indication of how well an architecture is suited for an application (that is, a test program) is the amount of memory needed to represent it. $S_{i,j,k}$ was defined as the number of 8-bit bytes of memory used by programmer i to represent test program j in the machine language of architecture k. The S measure includes all instructions, indirect addresses, and temporary work areas required by the program. The only memory requirement not included in S is the memory needed to hold the actual data structures, or parameters, specified for use by the test programs.

Processor Execution-Rate Measures

In selecting among computer architectures—as opposed to alternative computer systems—one of the most basic measures of a computer is the speed with which it can solve problems. Yet a computer architecture is an abstract description of a computer that does not define the time required to perform any operation. The M and R measures were developed to measure those aspects of a computer architecture that would most directly affect the performance of its implementations.

Processor-Memory Transfers

If there is any single, scalar quantity that comes close to measuring the power of a computer system, it is the bandwidth between primary memory and the central processor(s) [2,4,5]. This measure is not concerned with the internal workings of either the primary memory or the central processor; it is determined by the width of the bus between primary memory and the processor and the number of transfers per second the bus is capable of sustaining. Since processor-memory bandwidth is a good indicator of a computer's execution speed, an important measure of an architecture's effect on the execution speed of a program is the amount of information it must transfer between primary memory and the processor during the execution of the program. If one architecture must read or write 2×10^6 bytes in primary memory in order to execute a test program and the second architecture must read or write 10^6 bytes in order to execute the same test program, then, given similar implementation constraints, one would expect the second architecture to be substantially faster than the first.

The particular measure of primary-memory/central-processor transfers used by the committee is called the M measure. $M_{i,j,k}$ was defined as the number of 8-bit bytes that must be read or written from primary memory by the processor of computer architecture k

during the execution of test program j as written by programmer i.

Register Transfers within the Processor

The processor-memory traffic measure just described was the committee's principal measure of a computer architecture's execution rate performance, but the M measure does not capture all one wants to know about the performance potential of an architecture. A second measure of architecture performance was defined: R, register-to-register traffic within the processor. The M measure looks at the data traffic between primary memory and the central processor. R is a measure of the data traffic internal to the central processor. The fundamental goal of the M and R measures was to enable the committee to construct a processor execution-rate measure from M and R (ultimately an additive measure: $aM + bR$, where the coefficients a and b can be varied to model projections of relative primary memory and processor speeds). The R measure is very sensitive to assumptions about the register and bus structure internal to the processor—in other words, the implementation of the architecture. $R_{i,j,k}$ was defined as the number of 8-bit bytes that are read to and written from the internal processor registers during execution of test program j on architecture k as written by programmer i.

Evaluation

The test-program phase of the selection study involved an elaborate statistical design to eliminate bias due to programmers [2,3]. It evaluated the three architectures in the same order as the initial prefiltering—that is, Interdata 8/32, PDP-11, IBM System/370. The results of this study provoked considerable controversy among the military representatives, especially those from the Navy. They found the results of the quantitative criteria surprising because small-scale computers generally came out ahead of large-scale computers, whereas it had been assumed that the intent was to measure the power of each architecture. The following results from analysis of this situation. First, most minicomputers have a short word length and consequently a short address field for typical instructions. Therefore, it would be expected that criteria V1, V2, P1, P2, and D would show lower values for these computers. All these computers, however, provide one or more instruction classes (such as, RX) or subclasses that make use of two words per instruction, with a longer direct-address field; these special classes of instructions were used as the basis for the response to the initial CFA user survey. Large-scale processors, on the other hand, provide large address fields for the majority of instruction classes. Thus to be valid the survey should have specified the average effective values for these measures rather than allowing proponents to submit the best case value.

In terms of the criteria to be minimized (CS, CM, I, L, J), the small-scale processors came out ahead of the large-scale processors for several reasons:

1. The minicomputers came out ahead on measures CS2, CM2, L, and J because they were able to drop out registers and optional features. The large-scale processors were penalized on these measures because they provide many features as standard, even though subsetability was assumed. The minicomputers are able to include these optional features in some criteria but to omit them for others, to best advantage.

2. Relative to measure C, which relates to the size of the processor state, it is obvious that more powerful architectures have a larger state. One can verify this by reflecting on the fact that first-generation computers (ERA 1103, IBM 704, and so on) had very small processor states (only a single A register, MQ register, no base registers, few if any index registers, and so on). Yet the committee was giving

credit for minimizing the size of the processor state.

3. In connection with processor state, the directions for calculating measures CS and CS2 state that processors are assumed to resume at a later date. In a tactical environment, however, an interrupted process is never resumed at a later date. Advanced large-scale processors provide a capability for automatic context switching on interrupt, so that the number of registers that have to be stored in and retrieved from main memory to save and resume interrupted processes in a typical situation is zero. This factor was not considered in the evaluation criteria.

4. Criterion I, which measures I/O latency, was based on the premise that a single byte was being input or output. Again, this is a typical situation and one that favors small-scale processors.

To compound the bias toward small-scale computers introduced by the foregoing factors, some considered the method selected for normalizing the criteria to be minimized statistically unsound. The results were derived by taking the reciprocals of values CS, CM, I, L, and J and normalizing them as follows: the arithmetic mean of these reciprocals is taken across the set of architectures, then divided into each reciprocal to produce the normalized value. This technique biases the results toward extreme values. The use of geometric rather than arithmetic mean would have been more appropriate here.

The importance attached to the criteria to be minimized outweighs that of those to be maximized. This is due to the compounding effect of the weighting of the minimized measures (51.2 percent total) and the bias caused by improper normalization. The net effect is a bias toward small architectures.

No credit was given for features of a powerful architecture such as indirect addressing, independent I/O controllers, multilevel interrupt structures, or double-precision arithmetic.

On the basis of the criteria used and the way in which they were normalized and weighted, the ideal architecture would appear to have the following characteristics:

1. Large fixed instructions composed of an overlarge opcode field and a very large address field.

2. No index or arithmetic registers—all operations to and from memory.

3. Only sufficient base and protection registers to meet absolute criteria.

4. Simple I/O, oriented toward input and output of single bytes.

5. No standard features—all instructions, registers, and so on optional.

The critics of the committee's selection process point out somewhat sarcastically that the foregoing could probably be met by a detuned IBM 705 or 1401, and question whether that is really what the Army and Navy need in the period from the 1980s to 1990.

Final Outcome

The concept of a software-compatible family of computers based on instruction-set architecture drawn from the commercial world has great appeal for the following reasons:

1. Software transportability over family members.

2. Capture of the extensive commercial support software.

3. Wide programmer familiarity.

4. Life-cycle cost savings.

5. Risk reduction through pursuit of state of the art rather than advancement of it.

An issue of concern to some was that one family might not suffice for all Navy applications, for example. Several committee members suggested that a more realistic approach would be to have two families: a low-end 16-bit and a high-end 32-bit family architecture. Other issues of concern were whether old commercial architectures will meet future requirements in the areas of security and fault-tolerance. Moreover, the restriction of the architecture selection to the processor architectures rather than total-system architecture left many issues unresolved (such as what type and mix of processors, type of memory hierarchies or networks, interconnection philosophy, and the like will be required in future Navy systems). The resulting vagueness in the bussing structure is only one sympton of the failure to consider broader system-architecture issues.

Many groups reviewing the committee's selection expressed dissatisfaction; the principal concern was that what started as one ISA family has evolved into a family of hardware modules for many ISAs. The review group did not think the same hardware architecture partitioning could be performance-or cost-effective over four ISAs of different performance levels. Furthermore, the addition of two Navy architectures (UYK-7 to UYK-20) to the Army's four would further compound the problem.

Other areas of concern expressed by review-group members are the following:

1. The selection of many ISAs runs counter to good product-line-development strategy since support-software costs are multiplied.

2. The committee plans to standardize on the wrong level of hardware. At the module level, technology insertion is limited. In five or ten years even the best current modular design will not be cost-effective compared with new technology.

3. Multisourcing at the board/module level of high-complexity equipment is unproved and risky.

4. There was a real question as to the ability of the then top-of-the-line processor architecture (PDP-11/70) to provide a replacement for the Navy's standard tactical computer, the AN/UYK-7.

5. The fact that one of the three finalists did not meet the original absolute requirements caused concern.

Considering the ground rules and charter laid down at the time, the committee's selection process was about as thorough as could be expected. Time and money constraints resulted in an inability to consider many issues in detail. It has been argued that the selection process favored 16-bit (over 32-bit) architectures. The selection process also favored uniprocessor architectures at the expense of multiprocessor architectures. Thus the PDP-11, which had a moderately good score on most measures, was selected. A very important criterion to many committee representatives was the availability of a licensing agreement with a moderate royalty structure. Here again the PDP-11 looked best.

A large majority of the review group's members concurred with the selection of the PDP-11 architecture for at least a low-end family. The committee's final decision, however, was that any of the three finalists was suitable as a family architecture for all levels. It was noted that the PDP-11 had one flaw that needed correction—namely, its very limited virtual-address space. DEC promised an extension and came through with the VAX-11/780, a substantially expanded architecture from the PDP-11. It is basically a 32-bit architecture for large central-computer applications; it has little direct upward architectural compatibility from the PDP-11 (that is, a subset of the task-state instructions). Instead, it may be viewed as a dual-mode machine or a machine with a PDP-11 emulation mode. One might view DEC's transition from the PDP-11 to the VAX as iconic since it was evaluated and chosen as a 16-bit architecture. The selection criteria allowed minimal changes to the chosen architecture. The original goal of the computer family architecture-selection process is to select as a base architecture a commercial architecture that is in widespread use with a large software and experience base. Thus from the point of view of requirements-oriented system design, if the goal was as stated just previously, then the selection process—however well-motivated and expertly carried out—missed the mark. On the other hand, if requirements orientation meant evaluation of existing tactical data-processing systems that were performing against current requirements, then the committee evaluation failed, since these machines failed to meet the absolute criteria of the first phase of the study.

We chose this case study because of an even stranger irony than the 16-or 32-bit transmutation of the chosen ISA. If the initial goal had been perfectly met, and if the concept of architecture employed and transcended the ISA to include the entire hardware system—and, further, the entire software tradition of that architecture, captured intact—the selection *still would not have succeeded*. At the same time, the very agencies funding this architecture selection were developing a radical, sophisticated new software approach to tactical data processing, which emerged shortly after the computer-family architecture selection as the Ada language and its environment. Thus the software tradition so cleverly captured would have been of little value anyway; and many questioned whether commercial software would have any value for tactical or command, control, and communications in any case.

The reader may be asking what the moral of this story is. Perhaps it is that in computer architecture, as in building architecture, *one can stand too close to one's subject to appreciate its overall complexity*. After all, computer architecture is more than instruction-set archi-tecture. The analyst, however, is tempted to focus too closely on the aspect of his subject that is most easily quantified. If a system is more than the sum of its parts—and if analysis is a process by which we seek to understand complex systems by breaking them into their constituent parts for more convenient study—then analysis is unlikely to help us understand whatever it is about a system that is more than the sum of its parts.

References

1. Burr, W.E.; Coleman, A.H.; and Smith, W.R. "Overview of the Military Computer Family Architecture Selection." *Proceedings of the National Computer Conference* (1977): 132-137.

2. Fuller, S.H., and Burr, W.E. "Measurement and Evaluation of Alternative Computer Architectures." *Computer* (October 1977): 24-35.

3. Fuller, S.H.; Shaman, P.; Lamb, D.; and Burr, W.E. "Evaluation of Computer Architectures via Test Programs." *Proceedings of the National Computer Conference* (1977): 147-160.

4. Bell, C.G., and Newell, A. *Computer Structures: Readings and Examples*. New York: McGraw-Hill, 1971.

5. Stone, H.S., ed. *Introduction to Computer Architecture*. Chicago: Science Research Associates, 1975.

APPENDIX E

An Interim-Successor Architecture Design

Historical Significance

The historical importance of the requirement study described in this Appendix is that it is one of the best (if not the best) examples, of which we are aware, of the selecting the design of a simple multiple processor system.

Current applicability of this Appendix is for designers of real time systems or simple processor systems such as those used in advanced process control systems. There are a number of manufacturers of chip sets in the embedded processing area whose products could be used in this type of a system.

While the architectural-selection process described in Appendix D was underway, one of the participating agencies developed a critical performance problem in certain real-time multiprocessor applications. The application requirements were sufficiently critical to provoke a design study for an interim system that could meet them. The system-architecture design study presented here is a case history of how a truly requirement-oriented design can be accomplished efficiently for a balanced system with mature hardware, software, and application program components with maximal performance gain at minimal cost to the system in design, manufacture, complexity, and reconfiguration.

A series of computer performance studies were carried out as part of the interim successor-hardware design to improve the performance of a multiprocessor system by a factor of 4, as measured in a particular application for which the current system was highly stressed [1]. Thus this design was both motivated by a critical requirements problem and constrained by the history of the system and software it was to succeed. Two major architectural alternatives were considered:

- the inclusion of an additional parallel processor to handle part of the computation, and

- a speedup option in the current processor unit.

The first alternative would provide considerable performance gain in the one application, but its value in other situations was questionable. The second alternative could have the advantage of minimum disturbance of the current system architecture and could even be designed to be transparent to existing system and application software. An effort was thus undertaken to design an improved processor unit and to match the speed of this new processor to that of the installed memory units by means of a cache or buffer memory [2,3,4].

The architectural alternatives considered for cache organization included a memory-oriented design having a cache as a new top level in the memory hierarchy; a processor-oriented design having a small cache dedicated to each processor in the system; and a system-oriented design with the cache acting as an independent system module between the processor units and the memory units. The processor-oriented design was chosen because it afforded the least disturbance to the current architecture; in fact, it could be implemented by changing or redesigning the processor unit alone, leaving memory, input/output, and power units without significant modification [5].

The design goal thus became that of providing a 4-times increase in system performance by redesigning only the processor unit.

Modeling studies were carried out to see how well the projected designs would meet the improvement objectives, and to aid logic designers in taking the most cost-effective of several design alternatives. Since initial modeling efforts showed that performance would likely fall short of the intended 4-times goal, refinements were made in the model in an attempt to ensure that all the performance-enhancement potential of the design was being accounted for in the model. A comparison of the result from the various performance calculations gives some indication of the value of a simple model, compared with a more refined, costly, and complex model—each designed to predict the performance of the same configuration.

The system under study is the multiprocessor shown in Figure E-1. It consists of one to three processors, each having 0.5 million instructions per second (MIPS) execution rate; one or two input/output processors, each having a 0.1 MIPS capability; and one to sixteen memory modules to 16K-bit words each. The memory-cycle time is 1.5 microseconds, and each memory module has two access ports. The system allows interlaced memory addressing, and the processors are able to overlap instruction and operand fetches. This computer finds application in a wide variety of different configurations in real-time application environments. The high degree of modularity of the architecture encourages the selection of highly application-tailored configurations. The smaller of these range from a system with one processor (CPU), one I/O processor (IOP), and only four or five memory units, to a three-CPU, two-IOP configuration with twelve or more memory units. A few special-purpose applications may require larger configurations—for example, four CPUs, four IOPs and sixteen memory units. These large configurations are not general purpose, however, as they exceed the architectural scale of the system since all processors are no longer able to address all memory units.

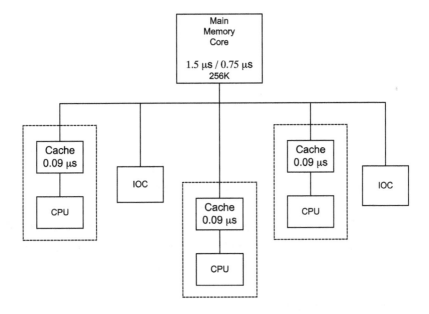

Figure E-1: CPU-oriented cache architecture

The processor-oriented cache architecture was thus chosen over memory-or system-oriented alternatives because it required the least change in the system as a whole. In principle, only the processor unit itself would have to be redesigned. The design alternatives within this general choice included a number of possibilities, which were evaluated using performance models at several levels of detail or fidelity to the design. The design alternatives considered for the processor-oriented cache included a variety of cache organizations and sizes. Cache sizes included 256, 1,024, 2,048, and 4,096 words, organized into from one to eight sets. A number of fetch, placement, and replacement policies were considered.

Block fetches with blocks of two and four words were considered, but primary consideration was given to four-word demand (demand based on a reference to any of the four words in the block), with the processor delayed until all four words have arrived in the cache. A modified four-word demand strategy under which the two words that include the processor reference are fetched first (such that the processor may continue in parallel with the fetch of the other pair of words in the block), and a two word look-ahead mode under which reference to a word of a block automatically causes a request for the next consecutive block, were also modeled.

The fetched block is placed in the cache using an available set if one can be found that does not contain a valid entry. If none can be found, the replacement policy determines the placement. Two bits are used to record usage information, such that when necessary, a fetched block replaces the block with the most remote reference time. This scheme is the familiar least-recently-used (LRU) policy.

The simplest model of processor-oriented cache performance can be derived from a knowledge of memory and cache speeds (access times) and an assumed hit rate (the ratio of words requested by the processor to the number of requests satisfied without a reference to memory). Such a simple model is often quoted [2], is considered quite useful, and yields the average access time as the performance measure. Specifically, average access time is given by:

Average Read Cycle time = (Cache Cycle Time)(Hit Rate) +
(Main Memory Cycle Time)(1-Hit Rate)

Assuming a cache cycle time of 180 nanoseconds and a main memory cycle of 1.5 microseconds per word or 2.5 per overlapped four-word block, this model yields an expected-read performance as shown in Table E-1.

Hit Rate	Average Read Cycle	Performance Cycle
0.90	0.412	3.64
0.91	0.389	3.86
0.92	0.365	4.10
0.93	0.342	4.38
0.94	0.319	4.70
0.95	0.296	5.06

Table E-1. Expected-Read Performance

Although the model does give some insight into the effect of including a cache, it is misleading in that it equates average access time with processor speed.

When a cache is placed in a system that is otherwise unaltered, the average access time cannot be equated with processor speed because the system does not run at cache speed. Specifically, inclusion of a cache redistributes the number of—and operation codes for—so-called extended-sequence instructions (instructions requiring processor time in excess of a memory cycle). To overcome this deficiency, the model can be extended by dividing the repertoire of the machine into four classes: instructions requiring an operand, instructions not requiring an operand, store instructions, and jump instructions. Statistical data from a large body of application programs allowed estimation of the unconditional probability that an instruction was from each class. On the basis of these classes, one can produce models to estimate the average instruction-execution time for each cache architecture. This approach provides a better indicator of total system performance.

The performance ratios calculated from the extended model are given in Tables E-2, E-3, and E-4. They are all based on the current core-memory processor, which has an average instruction time of 2.197 microseconds.

Data Hit Rate	92	94	Code Hit Rate 95	96	98
90	2.76	2.83	2.87	2.91	2.99
95	3.05	3.13	3.17	3.22	3.32
100	3.40	3.50	3.56	3.61	3.74

Table E-2: Performance Ratios for Four-Word Demand with Buffered Write-Through

Data Hit Rate	92	94	Code Hit Rate 95	96	98
90	3.06	3.43	3.15	3.19	3.26
95	3.25	3.48	3.36	3.40	3.48
100	3.43	3.52	3.56	3.60	3.69

Table E-3: Performance Ratios for Modified Four-Word Demand with Buffered Write Through

The desired operating point was at the 95-percent hit-rate level for both instructions and data. For this level the models compare as follows:

Architecture	Performance
Current processor with core memory	1.00
Four word demand and buffered write through (WT)	3.17
Two-word look ahead and buffered WT	3.47
Modified four-word demand and buffered WT	3.36

These figures are for a typical workload chosen from actual applications. In summary, the simple model estimates a 5.06-times improvement at the 95-percent hit-ratio level whereas the best extended model predicts a 3.47-times improvement at the 95-percent hit-ratio level. The two estimates are clearly not compatible, but the situation was resolved by detailed simulation study. Actual typical application code and produced trace tapes continuing a record of instruction addresses, instruction codes, and operand addresses were prepared. A simulator program read the trace tapes and calculated performance of a cache-equipped system. The simulated programs were also run on the current equipment and their execution times recorded.

Data Hit Rate	92	94	Code Hit Rate 95	96	98
90	3.20	3.23	3.25	3.25	3.30
95	3.41	3.45	3.47	3.48	3.52
100	3.61	3.66	3.68	3.70	3.74

Table E-4: Performance Ratios for Two-Word Look Ahead with Buffered Write-Through

Thus validation by comparison was facilitated for the single-processor configuration. The cache-oriented simulator was very detailed and properly accounted for instruction operand fetch overlap, multi-instructions per word, the cache, the read-write busses, the buffered write-through components and the interleaved memory modules. Considerable care was taken to ensure that all activity timing and component synchronization were properly represented.

The result of the simulation study showed that a cache-equipped system will reach a performance of 3.5 times that of the current system when executing actual code from typical applications. This result confirmed the result of the model, which included second-order effect, and was a disappointment to those hoping for a clear 4-times improvement over a CPU-only change to the system. Further study showed that a memory redesign would also be required to obtain a factor-of-4 improvement but would reduce overall cost-performance of the interim system significantly. Though not the desired result, a guaranteed factor-of-3.5 performance improvement for the intended application by charging only the CPU component of the system is a strong result and an interesting example of requirements-oriented system (re)design at the hardware-architecture level.

References

1. Patton, P.C.; Franta, W.R.; Petschauer, T.W.; and Pliml, R.F.; "On Performance Studies of Processor Oriented Cache Configurations." Workshop for Computing System Models, Institute fur Informatik, University of Bonn, Federal Republic of Germany, March 1977.

2. Liptay, J.S. "Structural Aspect of the System/360 Model 85: II. The Cache." IBM System Journal 7, no. 1 (1968): 15-21.

3. Bell, O.J.; Casasent, D.; and Bell, C.G.; "An Investigation of Alternative Cache Organizations." IEEE Transactions on Computers (April 1974): 346-351.

4. Pohm, A.V.; Agrawal, O.P.; and Monroe, R.N.; "The Cost of Performance Tradeoffs of Buffered Memories." IEEE Proceedings 63, no. 8 (August 1975): 1129-1135.

www.ingramcontent.com/pod-product-compliance
Lightning Source LLC
Chambersburg PA
CBHW071202050326
40689CB00011B/2215